CW00349096

Renewing the Eucharist
Volume 1

Journey

Renewing the Eucharist

Series editor: Stephen Burns

Volumes planned

1 *Journey*
GATHERING Richard Giles
WORD Nicola Slee
TABLE Ann Loades
SENDING Mark Ireland

2 *Word*
HEBREW SCRIPTURE Jo Bailey-Wells
PSALMS Gordon Mursell
NEW TESTAMENT Joy Tetley
GOSPELS Andrew Gregory

3 *Table*
TAKING Lizette Larson-Miller
BLESSING David Stancliffe
BREAKING Alan Bartlett
GIVING John B. Thomson

4 *Prayer*
PRAISE Mark Earey
THANKSGIVING Stephen Platten
CONFESSION Harriet Harris
INTERCESSION John Pritchard

5 *Time*
CHRISTMAS CYCLE David Runcorn
EASTER CYCLE Ruth A. Meyers
ORDINARY TIME Ellen Clark-King
THE SAINTS Mark Pryce

for further information visit
www.canterburypress.co.uk

RENEWING THE EUCHARIST
Volume 1

Journey

Richard Giles, Nicola Slee,
Ann Loades and Mark Ireland

Series Editor:
Stephen Burns

CANTERBURY
PRESS
Norwich

© The Contributors 2008

First published in 2008 by the Canterbury Press Norwich
Editorial office
13–17 Long Lane, London EC1A 9PN

Canterbury Press is an imprint of Hymns Ancient and Modern Ltd
(a registered charity)
St Mary's Works, St Mary's Plain,
Norwich, NR3 3BH, UK

www.scm-canterburypress.co.uk

All rights reserved. No part of this publication may be reproduced, stored in a retrieval system, or transmitted, in any form or by any means, electronic, mechanical, photocopying or otherwise, without the prior permission of the publisher, Canterbury Press.

The Authors have asserted their right under the Copyright, Designs and Patents Act, 1988, to be identified as the Authors of this Work

Scripture quotations are from the New Revised Standard Version of the Bible, © 1989 by the Division of Christian Education of the National Council of the Churches of Christ in the USA, as found in *Readings for the Assembly, Revised Common Lectionary Cycles A, B and C*, edited by Gordon W. Lathrop and Gail Ramshaw, copyright © 1995, 1996 and 1997 by Augsburg Fortress Press.

Copyright material is quoted from the following ritual resources, for which permission to use here is gratefully received: *Common Worship: Services and Prayers for the Church of England* (2000: pp. x, 27, 171, 182, 332, 540); *Common Worship: Christian Initiation* (2005: pp. 68, 73); *Common Worship: Daily Prayer* (2005: p. 223); *Evangelical Lutheran Worship* (2006: p. 115); *Gathering for Worship* (2005: p. 21); and *The Methodist Worship Book* (1999: pp. 51, 197).

British Library Cataloguing in Publication data

A catalogue record for this book is available from the British Library

ISBN 978-1-85311-860-9

Typeset by Regent Typesetting, London
Printed in the UK by CPI Bookmarque, Croydon, CR0 4TD

Contents

Acknowledgements

This series began life in Birmingham, England, while I was Tutor in Liturgy at the Queen's Foundation for Ecumenical Theological Education. It was completed in Sydney, Australia, where I am now Research Fellow in Public and Contextual Theology at United Theological College in Charles Sturt University. Both colleges host impressive Christian communities and I count myself blessed to have found myself in very good company in each place. Moreover, from the inclusive and collaborative disciplines they share, I hope to have learned both vision and practices for my own life of faith and ministry.

I am grateful to Christine Smith at SCM-Canterbury Press for her support of this series, as well, of course, to those who have written for it. Thank you also to Linda Foster, Mary Matthews and Jill Wallis for their work on the production of this book. And my thanks are also, as ever, due to Judith and Dominic who bring strength and delight to my daily life.

Stephen Burns

Renewing the Eucharist
Orientation to the series

1 Journey 2 Word 3 Table
4 Prayer 5 Time

Renewing the Eucharist is a short series of small books on eucharistic spirituality. Each book offers concise, focused theological explorations of key liturgical themes intended to invite a readership across and beyond the Church of England. Now that the Church's *Common Worship* resources for the eucharist are authorized and employed in parishes, the *Renewing the Eucharist* series is a timely resource to help foster deepening liturgical formation of worshippers.

There are five volumes in the *Renewing the Eucharist* series. Each one consists of:

- an introductory essay by the editor,
- four thematic essays of 5,000 words each by leading thinkers on the key topic,
- a note on constructing lectionary sequences that will help to bring the themes of *Renewing the Eucharist*

into preaching as part of eucharistic celebration, and
- some questions for thought for individual readers, or for conversation where the book is read in small groups.

Writers of the individual chapters present a core concern of theirs in a handful of pages, in accessible, non-technical language. 'What is the heart of this subject?' is the essential question they aim to address. Juxtaposed one to another, they aim to animate the connections between celebrating the eucharist and faithful Christian living, so that the spiritual practices of readers may be refreshed and emboldened.

The writers themselves come from a wide range of 'church styles' and theological traditions within the Church of England, with several writing from locations further afield. Each one writes from their own convictions; and the differences between them, as well as what they share, invite readers to refresh their own perspective on the journey through the liturgy, the central things of word and table, the modes and moods of prayer, and the unfolding of time – all gifts of grace.

The journey through the liturgy

STEPHEN BURNS

A structure with signposts

This first volume of the *Renewing the Eucharist* series explores the basic way the Church of England's 'Order for the Celebration of Holy Communion' is shaped.[1] It takes its lead from the Preface to *Common Worship*, which states:

> The journey through the liturgy has a clear structure with signposts for those less familiar with the way. It moves from the gathering of the community through the Liturgy of the Word to an opportunity of transformation, sacramental or non-sacramental, after which those present are sent out to put their faith into practice.[2]

1 See *Common Worship: Services and Prayers for the Church of England*, 2000, London: Church House Publishing, p. 155, which refers to 'The Order for the Celebration of Holy Communion also called The Eucharist and The Lord's Supper'. In the following notes, the 'Sunday book' of *Common Worship* is referred to as *Common Worship*; other volumes in the Common Worship series are referred to with their subtitle.

2 *Common Worship*, p. x.

This volume, *Journey*, is intended not only for those who may be unfamiliar with the shape of eucharistic celebration, but also for those for whom the structure is well known, in the hope that what is read here will deepen appreciation and understanding.

The Preface for *Common Worship* itself reflects a wider view, in that an emphasis on a fourfold 'flow' from gathering to word to table to sending is one of the key ways in which contemporary ecumenical consensus is expressed. The World Council of Churches has affirmed that, liturgically, holy communion consists of:

> GATHERING of the assembly into the grace, love and *koinonia* [communion] of the triune God.
>
> WORD-SERVICE
>
> > Reading of the scriptures of the Old and New Testaments
> > Proclaiming Jesus Christ crucified and risen as the ground of our hope
> > (and confessing and singing our faith)
> > and so interceding for all in need and for unity
> > (sharing the peace to seal our prayers and prepare for the table)
>
> TABLE-SERVICE
>
> Giving thanks over bread and cup
>
> and so
>
> BEING SENT (DISMISSAL) in mission in the world[3]

The Roman Catholic order for mass is also shaped around the same four basic parts of the service, as is the celebration of holy communion in many Protestant traditions. Among these, the British *Methodist Worship Book* is perhaps especially interesting in that it not only expresses the four-fold ecumenical pattern in what it calls 'The gathering of the people of God', 'the ministry of the Word', 'the Lord's Supper' and 'prayers and dismissal', it also shapes its services of the word with a distinct echo of the same eucharistic shape. In its services of the word, gathering rites and ministry of the word lead to what is usually called a 'response', but that response intentionally includes 'thanksgiving' in a conscious echo of thanksgiving raised up in eucharistic prayer in the communion orders.[4] And within the Church of England itself, David Stancliffe, the chairperson of the Liturgical Commission at the time during which the *Common Worship* eucharist was introduced, taught his own lively way to imagine the traditional four-fold pattern, developing attractive correlations between the four parts of the eucharistic service and the dynamic notions of engaging (gathering), attending (the

3 Cited here from Thomas F. Best and Dagmar Heller, eds, 1995, *Eucharistic Worship in Ecumenical Contexts: The Lima Liturgy – and Beyond*, Geneva: World Council of Churches, p. 35.

4 1999, *Methodist Worship Book*, Peterborough: Methodist Publishing House, pp. 32 and 44, where thanksgiving forms part of 'the response'; also p. 51 where we read as the first point relating to the response in guidance for ordering a morning, afternoon or evening service that 'prayers of thanksgiving are offered for God's gift of creation in Christ through the Holy Spirit'.

word-service), transforming (the table-service), and energizing (sending out).[5] What is more, he also traced the significance of the pattern into other dimensions of liturgical celebration, for instance, thinking creatively about links with the liturgical seasons:

> The gathering or preparation [is] the advent or time of preparation in our worship, when we long for God's coming and tune our ears and eyes to recognize his presence . . .
>
> The Liturgy of the Word [is] the moment of Christmas, or celebration of the Word made flesh, coming among us to engage with us . . .
>
> The Liturgy of the Sacrament [is] God's transforming of our life by taking it into the passion and resurrection of Jesus Christ's dying and rising . . .
>
> The Dismissal [is] the moment of Pentecost, when the scattered disciples finally realized that God had given them all they needed to engage in their apostolic mission . . .[6]

The fourfold flow of eucharistic celebration, which *Common Worship* shares in common with the rites of many other traditions, is itself deeply indebted to the witness of what is the earliest extant description of eucharistic celebration in the early church. Justin Martyr writes about Sunday morning in Rome around AD 150 like this:

5 David Stancliffe, 2003, *God's Pattern: Shaping our Worship, Ministry and Life*, London: SPCK.

6 Stancliffe, *God's Pattern*, pp. 18–20.

> On the day named after the sun all, whether they live in the city or the countryside, are gathered together in unity. Then the records of the apostles or the writings of the prophets are read for as long as there is time. When the reader has concluded, the presider in a discourse admonishes and invites us into the pattern of these good things. Then we all stand together and offer prayer. And, as we said before, when we have concluded the prayer, bread is set out to eat, together with wine and water. The presider likewise offers up prayer and thanksgiving, as much as he can, and the people sing out their assent saying the amen. There is a distribution of the things over which thanks have been said and each person participates, and these things are sent by the deacons to those who are not present. Those who are prosperous and who desire to do so, give what they wish, according to each one's own choice, and the collection is deposited with the presider. He aids orphans and widows, those who are in want through disease or through another cause, those who are in prison, and foreigners who are sojourning here. In short, the presider is a guardian to all those who are in need . . .[7]

Justin was writing to the emperor Antoninus Pius and his purpose was primarily apologetic, commending the life of the community of faith to those outside it. It is not

---

7 Justin Martyr, *1 Apology* 67; this translation from Gordon W. Lathrop, 1993, *Holy Things: A Liturgical Theology*, Minneapolis, MN: Fortress Press, pp. 31–2.

clear to us whether his account is idealized – in order to create the best possible impression – whether it is a description of a 'one-off' event that varied from week to week, or whether it is the embedded and regular pattern of worship for a community. Nor is it clear whether what happened in Rome (or Justin's part of it) was related to what happened in other churches at the time. All this notwithstanding, Justin's record – as the earliest of any we have – is commonly regarded as of great significance for providing insight into the liturgical practice of at least some early Christians (the only ones we know about!). And it seems to be in continuity with key biblical witness, which depicts worship on Sunday, the first day of the week (cf. Acts 20.9); and, most importantly, in terms of involving attention to word and a meal at table. From among the gospels' many memories of Jesus' preaching and the mealtimes he shared, think especially of the risen one's encounter with disciples on the road to Emmaus: on the journey, Jesus opens the meaning of the scriptures (Luke 24.27) and makes himself known in the breaking of bread (Luke 24.35), and these actions are, of course, in continuity with a 'career' of preaching and companionship at table. Jesus' opening of the scriptures and ministry at tables has led many liturgical theologians, among countless other Christian people, to affirm that word and table are gifts of divine self-giving, means of grace through which God-in-Christ is made known in generous self-revelation.

Gathering, word, table, sending

Richard Giles writes the first chapter of *Journey* on the first part of the flow of the liturgy: gathering. Richard writes as the recently retired Dean of Philadelphia Cathedral, a building worth knowing about, not least for the ways in which, under Richard's leadership, it has boldly accented the importance of journey through the liturgy. Richard has written about the building in his book *Creating Uncommon Worship*,[8] which is itself a focused elaboration on his guide to 're-ordering the church building for worship and mission', *Re-pitching the Tent*.[9] Eucharistic celebration at the cathedral begins with gathering rites around the font, itself the place of beginnings in Christian life, then moves to seating around an ambo (or lectern) from where the word is read and proclaimed and responses in creed and prayer are offered, before it then moves again to a large open space around the altar-table for the communion meal itself. What is so striking about this is that the movement from one part of the building to another is not simply undertaken by the clergy and others leading, but by the whole assembly encouraged to regard themselves as a 'pilgrim people'. During the liturgy, the people of God are quite literally on the move, journeying together from one

8 Richard Giles, 2004, *Creating Uncommon Worship: Transforming the Liturgy of the Eucharist*, Norwich: Canterbury Press.

9 Richard Giles, 2004, *Re-pitching the Tent: The Definitive Guide to Re-ordering Church Buildings for Worship and Mission*, Norwich: Canterbury Press, third edition.

place to another where the Christian people gain their identity, receive nourishment and are commissioned and resourced for their diverse ministries and service within and beyond the gathered community. What has been possible in the Philadelphia liturgy is a challenge to the rest of us wherever we are, in whatever kind of space we gather, to *enact* the journey which the liturgy invites. Richard's writings are full of ideas about how this might happen, even in what may seem the unlikeliest of places, and he is insistent that people's participation in the eucharist can be renewed with little more than sheer determination to let it happen, given the necessary openness to change, which is part of that determination. So, then, Richard is the perfect person to launch our reflections in the context of this book on journey. In his chapter, he turns the notion of 'gathering' to pick up different strands of biblical resonance, stresses our gathering in Christian assembly as an act of witness in the midst of God's world, and makes a range of practical suggestions about how we might animate our gathering rites and the space in which they take place.

As we journey further into the book, we encounter **Nicola Slee**'s profound reflections on many dimensions of that rich, loaded descriptor, 'word'. In her teaching over years in the context of training persons for lay and ordained ministries (at the Aston Training Scheme and latterly the Queen's Foundation, Birmingham), Nicola has combined her gifts as both theologian and poet, making her a most interesting person to address this topic. As her recent books of prayers and poems, *Praying*

Like a Woman[10] and *The Book of Mary*,[11] so evidently suggest, she is one who loves words, and knows their beauty and power. But, particularly from the conscience afforded her as a feminist theologian, Nicola also knows the potential of words to hurt and damage, making clear in her contribution here that even the honoured words of sacred scripture and Christian tradition can be and are sometimes deeply ambiguous and need to be treated with the greatest of care. Like Richard Giles, Nicola makes a number of practical suggestions in her piece, in her case about how we might invite a lively care for word in our liturgical assemblies. And she does this not least by calling attention to embodied practices that complement Richard's emphasis on moving bodies around the building – so Nicola reflects, for example, on standing, on silence and on sight and how they each may help us engage the divine word. Her chapter beautifully circles around both thought and practice, all the time inviting readers to stretch from the details of the Liturgy of the Word to the expression of a response of love to the living God who beckons us near. Within the *Renewing the Eucharist* series, Nicola's chapter also anticipates a later volume dedicated to exploration of the lectionary dynamics of reading scripture that shape the second step of the eucharistic service, as well as another volume on the modes and moods of prayer.

Just as Nicola's contribution prepares the way for a later volume of the *Renewing the Eucharist* series, so too does

10 Nicola Slee, 2004, *Praying Like a Woman*, London: SPCK.
11 Nicola Slee, 2007, *The Book of Mary*, London: SPCK.

Ann Loades' chapter on 'table'. For a later volume gives special attention to the particular actions of taking, blessing, breaking and giving at the heart of the communion rite itself – actions that enact the gospels' memories of Jesus' own actions at table and that we in turn recall in eucharistic prayer. Like Nicola Slee, Ann takes a wide view of her topic, although in Ann's case this means choosing to give relatively little attention to the details of specific liturgical practices. Instead, she gives space to a sustained invitation into a sacramental way of regarding life in the world as a precious divine gift. Ann is herself emerita professor of divinity at Durham University, where among other things she was pioneering in the revival of the study of the sacraments in academic theological contexts. Her work in this area includes the companion books *The Sense of the Sacramental*[12] and *Christ the Sacramental Word*,[13] and her contribution to *Renewing the Eucharist* adds to the many essays she has written on the subject of sacramentality.[14] Here, she brings to bear her wealth of learning into a vision of life

12 David Brown and Ann Loades, eds, 1995, *The Sense of the Sacramental: Movement and Measure in Art and Music, Place and Time*, London: SPCK.

13 David Brown and Ann Loades, eds, 1996, *Christ The Sacramental Word: Incarnation, Sacrament and Poetry*, London: SPCK.

14 Note especially Ann Loades, 2004, 'Finding New Sense in the Sacramental' in Geoffrey Rowell and Christine Hall, eds, *The Gestures of God: Explorations in Sacramentality*, London: Continuum, pp. 161–72, and Ann Loades, 2005, 'Sacramentality and Christian Spirituality' in Arthur G. Holder, ed., *The Blackwell Companion to Christian Spirituality*, Oxford: Blackwell, pp. 254–68.

graced by confidence in God's 'flesh-and-blood making [and] flesh-and-blood taking' in creation and incarnation – the manifestation of divine presence in the world at large and in the person of Christ in particular. Her essay on sacramentality therefore uses the key terms of Christian doctrine not only to address aspects of the controversial history of specific sacraments, but to sketch a way of relating reflection on sacramentality (a perhaps less familiar notion to some) with its 'virtually inexhaustible' application to the very heartlands of Christian faith. With the wide largesse of God in creation and incarnation in mind, Ann's essay beckons our attention to the importance of particular activities at table in our own and others' homes, as much as 'at church', and charges us to make connections between the context of creation and the 'public-ness', as it were, of the liturgy so that we might see the significance of Christian worship stretching way beyond what happens on Sunday mornings.

Mark Ireland introduces the fourth theme, 'sending', and in so doing explores a range of inter-relationships between worship and mission. Mark writes as a priest, presently immersed in parish ministry, who has also served as a diocesan missioner for Lichfield. Mark has also helped greatly to foster others' thinking about mission and evangelism through the like of his *Evangelism: Which Way Now?*[15] He does more of the

15 Mike Booker and Mark Ireland, 2005, *Evangelism: Which Way Now?* London: Church House Publishing, second edition.

same in his essay for *Journey*, relating his topic to pressing current concerns in the Church of England about 'mission-shaped' church and 'fresh expressions' of Christian community. Making links with other sacraments such as baptism and confirmation, and exploring the meaning of some different names (such as 'mass') for holy communion, Mark also relates a wealth of lived examples of accenting the sending with which readers can compare – and into which they can imagine – themselves and their own situations. The effect is to unsettle any assumption we might have about there being just one way of 'doing' the sending at the end of the liturgy; rather, Mark invites us to explore the kind of daring experiments through which deeper meanings might break into our consciousness.

One important point that ought to be made after this brief introduction to what each particular author offers is that we should be aware of the ways in which their themes collapse into each other. So, for example, Richard speaks of the need for 'gathering' to be a 'repeated motif' throughout the whole eucharistic celebration, all the way along the journey, as it were. And Nicola speaks of being arrested by a description of how words might be 'good enough to eat', one way of saying: sacramental. She then concludes her reflections with thinking about word 'enfleshed', divine enfleshment being a theme Ann takes up before she herself ends up with a particular stress on worshippers being sent and resourced for public service. Then in his turn, Mark traces outward turns throughout the liturgy, not least bringing us full circle by especially relating gathering and sending. All this is to say that while it is good to open ourselves to deepening understanding of the particular 'parts' of eucharistic celebration, these parts overlap in richly textured ways so that noting the dynamics of their interaction is important for the deepest appreciation.

Each of the contributors to *Journey* writes from their own experience and convictions, so that, despite their obvious shared concerns, there are at least five distinct voices to be found within the pages of this little book. And some readers will make their way through what they read in groups in which perhaps many other voices are heard. But even where readers read alone, the different approaches, experiences and convictions here invite us to find our own voice in relation to them. We need to bear in mind that however or with whomever we read, we might find that at times we are inspired, encouraged, challenged, even puzzled, by each other. And to that we might well say: 'Welcome to church!' For the part of each of the contributors to *Journey* at least, we each in our own way write to invite an animation of the depth and breadth of spirituality, a word Ann Loades in her chapter attractively defines as 'how human beings become their best "selves" in their response' to God's seeking of them.[16] If that happens, we have contributed to collective daring to believe that the journey through the liturgy is a journey towards the greater flourishing of our personal and public life, to the glory of God, for the life of the world.

16 Below, p. 67.

Gathering

RICHARD GILES

Looking back to my growing years in Birmingham just after World War Two, I thank God for two particular blessings: my parish church (St Giles', Sheldon), which nurtured me in faith and was my safe haven, and the local railway, the GWR (God's Wonderful Railway), which nurtured me in beauty and romance and kept me forever looking to new horizons westward.

One school holiday, a little posse of terribly innocent co-eds from Waverley Grammar School converged on Snow Hill Station one sunny morning for an expedition into Shropshire. With packed lunches and Mars bars at the ready we gathered excitedly in the station forecourt, having caught buses from different corners of the city. We caught the (steam) train to Wellington, and walked to the edge of the town to the beginning of the trail up the Wrekin – that wondrous little sugar-loaf mountain that sticks up unbelievably out of the Shropshire Plain. From the top we gazed westward where all the glories of the Marches and of Wales stretched before us. It was a perfect day, which I now look back to as one does to a tantalizing fragment of a dream that cannot be recaptured.

As in most things, it was the gathering, the anticipation, the excitement of our convergence that was the best part. Would the weather hold? Would my best pal get out of bed in time? Did we have enough money for unforeseen eventualities? Who would sit next to Marie? Would Bill ask Doreen out? (Oh my, don't those names give away our ages!)

That morning outside Snow Hill Station was a classic act of gathering – assembling at a pre-arranged venue to begin a journey, a journey in which delight was tinged, even spiced up, by nervousness, uncertainty, or apprehension. None of those present would have missed it for the world.

Gathering to make eucharist somehow feels like a new idea, maybe something that emerged from Vatican II[17] (remember that?), a pastime engaged in by progressives who read *The Guardian* and are keen on recycling. But gathering is, of course, as old as the hills – something we humans do as a matter of course, in primeval instinctive response to danger, or loneliness, or curiosity. As Christians, our gathering has many strands to it, but is chiefly about gathering to journey.

---

17 For those who may not know, Vatican II was the council of Roman Catholic bishops in the mid 1960s, and its first outcome, The Constitution on the Sacred Liturgy, is widely regarded as having greatly helped to renew the liturgy not only of Roman Catholic communities, but of many Protestant traditions in their turn, so taken (as many were) by the bishops' vision of worship.

Gathering to journey

The Preface to *Common Worship* reminds us that 'worship itself is a pilgrimage – a journey into the heart of the love of God'.[18] It is a journey that begins with 'the gathering of the community'.[19]

If we sixth formers hadn't gathered outside Snow Hill Station that morning, the journey could not have begun. Our assembling was the prerequisite of the whole day that unfolded thereafter. Woody Allen is credited with the dictum that 95 per cent of life is showing up; the rest kind of follows. Gathering to make eucharist is not dissimilar. Like members of a walking club assembling at a trail head to attempt an expedition on a scale not previously undertaken, when we assemble for the liturgy we are also attempting something that will stretch us, take us to our limits, be on a scale that proves to be just beyond our reach.

Richard Meux Benson, founder of the Cowley Fathers, taught that we should celebrate every eucharist believing that the domain of God could break through at any moment. If this is so, when we feel perfectly in control of the eucharistic liturgy, therefore, we could say our approach has veered from the path. Like those hikers

---

18 *Common Worship*, p. x. (Can a committee really have written the superb prose?!)

19 *Common Worship*, p. x. The heading within Order One is simply 'The Gathering', although it should be noted that, for example, 2002, *New Patterns for Worship*, London: Church House Publishing, uses variable headings for the four parts of the service.

tackling a trail that is two levels above their competence, butterflies in the stomach and nervous laughter are perfectly appropriate as we gather for the liturgy. We gather for a purpose, for a journey, with a high level of anticipation laced with a dash of trepidation. It is a gathering for forward movement: the assembling of landing forces on a beachhead. Nothing could be further from an action defined as an end in itself, as is sometimes said of worship; rather, that which is beyond beckons.

In all forms of gathering, one step is more important than all others: the initial decision to count oneself in. This may be at the moment of waking, deciding to get out of bed before it's too late to catch that train; or at a fork in the road where, after a moment of indecision, your car just seems to take you where you need to be of its own accord; or at a point in a conversation where somehow you find yourself saying, 'Sorry, I've got to go.'

There isn't a parish priest anywhere in the world who doesn't share the sentiments of Woody Allen's dictum as she or he surveys the faces of the faithful gathered for the Sunday Liturgy and tries so desperately hard to love the attendees with more energy than she or he despairs of the absentees.

If every Christian learned the secret of gathering, then everything else would follow. Gathering is the simple part. It doesn't require intelligence, or training, or a high spirituality score; anyone can do it, even the recovering latecomer. It just requires a simple act of will. The act of gathering is therefore in one sense the most important of the whole liturgy. It gets us there. At this point we sign in; we register for all that is to come. To miss it is to miss the opening speech, the introduction that makes sense of all that follows.

Gathering as preparation

If we, as the people of God called to make eucharist, don't first gather, then the journey doesn't begin, or at least it doesn't begin in any meaningful way. Gathering as a community to prepare ourselves to offer the liturgy is actually part of the fun. Like any event to which we look forward throughout the week, like any party about which there's a buzz of excitement, any occasion to which we count off the days, we can't wait to get there early with our friends and to build the anticipation and to revel in the sheer joy of it.

I would argue that if we are merely 'on time' for the liturgy, just slipping into our seat as the eucharist begins, then we are in fact late. For we have failed to allow time for the essential process of gathering together. In the greeting of our fellow pilgrims and co-workers, we revel in each other's company and prepare for all that is to follow in the liturgy. The curious phenomenon of people being consistently late for worship, thereby depriving themselves of any sense of beginning the journey (and being discourteous to everyone present let alone to God) will no doubt continue until we literally leave the station as the liturgy begins. Perhaps only if we hold all eucharistic liturgies on chartered trains will the meaning of gathering for worship finally take hold (though it has to be admitted this would make for some very strange liturgical spaces). The danger is that if we insist on being late, or no more than 'on time', it means that, deep down, the liturgy has become for us something to attend, to observe, to be connected to at one step removed, rather than something to be lived, or dived into, or struggled with.

Being late for such a worship event is a great shame simply because one would thereby deprive oneself of the best part, the gathering. For the gathering is not merely a prelude or introduction to the worship; we should imagine it as more of a springboard, from which the worshipper is put into a proper frame of heart and mind and launched into the dimension of the domain of God. The individual is therefore made ready for worship, to give God worth-ship by first receiving from fellow-worshippers a sense of his or her own worth. In the experience of gathering, the individual finds recognition, identity, and mutual love. Whatever life has thrown our way in the previous days, here in this place, in this activity, we are known, and cherished, and may thereby be healed. In gathering for worship we come home. That is why gathering is not merely a necessary stage we are required to go through before we can begin. It is an essential component of worship in all its aspects – theological, liturgical, social and emotional. Gathering reminds us who we are, and how rich and blessed we are in each other's company on the road that God sets before us. So if we want to discover the power of liturgy to engage and transform, if we want to know what the Preface to *Common Worship* means when it says our 'worship can take wing',[20] then we must work at assembling, at

20 *Common Worship*, p. x.

gathering, with renewed vigour and determination. To misquote Woody Allen, 95 per cent of liturgy will be found to be gathering. So I say: 'Let's do it and let's get it right.'

Leaning into the tradition

For people of faith, gathering has a particular ontological significance grounded in our Judeo-Christian scriptural tradition. This tradition has many dimensions to it in addition to that of gathering for journey.

Gathering out of exile

The Hebrew scriptures give us a very positive concept of God gathering God's people out of a hostile environment, or recalling them from dispersal, and restoring them to divine favour. Think Deuteronomy 30.4: 'Even if you are exiled to the ends of the world, from there the LORD your God will gather you, and from there he will bring you back.'

At the congregation of Shir Shalom, Woodstock, Vermont, on a summer evening in 2007, the Friday evening service to greet the *Shabbat* drew an assembly of both year-rounders and members with summer homes in the area. In addition, there was a sprinkling of Christians participating in a festival of liturgy and music at the local Episcopal church.

It was a beautiful July evening, sunlit after heavy rain and blessed with a double rainbow. The community celebrated not only its new building – a spacious light-filled structure recalling a northern New England barn, nestling among wooded hills – but also its new rabbi, their first ever resident pastor, fresh from seminary and radiant with love for God. The community brimmed over with pride and joy, and it showed in the manner of their gathering.

The parking lot was half-filled 30 minutes before the service. To arrive at the worship space everyone first passed through a large entrance hall in which food was laid out in readiness, proclaiming welcome. Once in the worship space, those entering encountered a community in celebration of gathering. Not for them the stage-whispered conversations beloved of Anglicans, nor the kneeling in prayer of the more pious. Instead, this was a room that buzzed with life and vigour, as friends renewed acquaintance with those not seen for a week or for a season, and embraced with equal warmth those they recognized as visitors. Chairs, not fixed benches or pews, provided the seating, so that people moved about freely, moving chairs aside if necessary to reach those they wanted to greet. It was an object lesson in gathering as a reunion of the faithful diaspora. Scattered by geography for the rest of the year, or by daily routine over the last seven days, or by a faith tradition differing from the prevailing religious culture, they simply delighted, even exulted, in their coming together.

As the *Shabbat* service moved into its early phases, the gathering spilled over into the liturgy itself, when the young rabbi asked that the microphone be passed through the assembly to allow every single person present to introduce themselves and, where appropriate, to share something special that had happened to them during the week. By this means, the embrace of the initial welcome was carried through into the worship and given liturgical form, first as both Jew and Christian thanked God for one another, and then as the scripture passages for the service were read aloud by members of the assembly, irrespective of faith tradition, as that task was passed, person to person along the rows of seats.

This is a community of faith that simply is wild about gathering. It does gathering 'in a big way'. Gathering almost becomes its *raison d'être,* its big thing, that by which it is identified. What follows liturgically might almost seem incidental, but this is not so. The sole reason for the community's gathering is to worship God, but on arrival it is repeatedly so knocked out by the convergence of kindred spirits and familiar faces and beloved friends, that it has no option but to give physical expression to this encounter.

The theme of gathering back together after exile, to restore and re-establish what had been lost, or scattered through disobedience, is a theme running right through the Hebrew scriptures, and is linked by the prophet Jeremiah to the concept of the faithful remnant, which has kept the flame of faith alive and is now to be rescued by God, after the catastrophe of Babylonian Exile: 'Then I myself will gather the remnant of my flock out of all the lands where I have driven them, and I will bring them back to their fold, and they shall be fruitful and multiply' (Jeremiah 23.3).

The community that gathered that evening in south-eastern Vermont were glad to see each other at many different layers of consciousness. They were glad to see each other as neighbours of the same locality, released from their daily routines to worship God; glad to see each other as residents of the same country, reunited for the summer season with those who lived the rest of the year in distant Florida; but also glad to see each other because, in the living memory of some of those present, especially those with German and East European names, you could never take for granted that you would ever see again the person who was alongside you only yesterday. For Jews, 'people of memory', as the young rabbi reminded them that night, history has been a long struggle for survival, which seems to have got worse, not better, as humankind has supposedly grown more 'civilized'. The awful dilemma for the Jewish person, struggling to be faithful, has always been that the very separation in which lay their distinctiveness and God's call, was at the same time the characteristic that provoked suspicion and hostility.

In the final stages of the journey out of the wilderness into the promised land of plenty, God promises that God's presence will go before God's people, and Moses sees in this blessing the distinctiveness of God's people: 'In this way, we shall be distinct, I and your people, from every people on the face of the earth' (Exodus 33.16). Such separation served to heighten both their sense of belonging to one another and the risks that such association brought them. Gathering for them was therefore always a two-edged sword; it was what kept them going and it was what might hasten their demise. No wonder there is electricity in the air when they get together!

Gathering in compassion

In gathering, we merely mimic God, who is the great gatherer. 'Gather into one all who share these holy mysteries' says the ancient eucharistic prayer known as *The Apostolic Tradition*. We stand around God's altar-table, as we look expectantly towards God, knowing of the divine track record for gathering of waifs and strays, sinners and saints.

When Jesus arrives at Jerusalem, the city he was at once both drawn to and dreaded, he speaks of gathering in terms of a compassionate protective love. His own love for the holy city, the centre of his own religious tradition, is an agonized *cri de coeur*, for he realizes that inevitably it must also be the place of his own demise: 'Jerusalem, Jerusalem, the city that kills the prophets and stones those who are sent to it! How often have I desired to gather your children together as a hen gathers her brood under her wings, and you were not willing!' (Matthew 23.37)

Those of us who, in response to overwhelming social problems that surround us, tend to despair or to bury ourselves in workshops rather than in Christian action, need to pay attention to the potential power of gathering for social change. When a community of faith gathers to make eucharist, we see before us, at least potentially, the accumulation of a critical mass, the mobilization of a peace-corps, the assembling of an army of co-workers, the creation of an unstoppable force.

Of course, the community requires prophetic leadership for this potential to be realized, for the community to know what it is, and the power given into its hands. Because prophets are in short supply, supportive leadership that does not quench the Spirit will often suffice. With such leadership, the voice within the community that tirelessly recalls us to the compassion of Christ in the face of suffering and despair, will be heard and responded to.

Gathering for eucharist provides us with the potential for communal action that can help transform society. We simply have to have our eyes and ears open, and our hearts and minds geared to respond.

Gathering for safety and solidarity

The concept of gathering a scattered and vulnerable population into fortified towns or villages where they can enjoy relative safety is familiar from the history of all societies. We gather for strength, mutual protection, and solidarity, whether behind the battlements of a fortress, or in a convoy of ships on a long sea crossing. There is safety in numbers we say, and we gather to amass those numbers. Little by little a collection of unsure, self-conscious and timid individuals undergoes an unavoidable change, as numbers swell, becoming a little army: exhilarated, buoyant and fearless, ready for anything.

Gregory Dix, in his classic *The Shape of the Liturgy,* digresses at one point from the minutiae of liturgical development to provide a splendid account of what it must have been like for Christians in persecution to gather to make eucharist. He transposes the scene from the Roman Empire of the second century to central

London in the twentieth century, and imagines the gathering of the church in that situation. The central figure is a 'grocer in Brondesbury, a tradesman in a small way of business', who sets out through the silent streets at 4.30 a.m. on what for the rest of the population is a normal working day, in order to make eucharist on the day of resurrection. The assembly point is the home of a wealthy woman near Hyde Park, where 'sitting in the best arm chair is an elderly man, a gentleman by his clothes but nothing out of the ordinary – the bishop of London'.[21]

Christians in many parts of the world today find themselves at odds with their prevailing culture, and can be painfully aware that exposure to discrimination and danger is part and parcel of the Christian calling. They are experiencing something of the danger known to so many previous generations of Christians.

This sometimes happens in the most unlikely places. The faith community of St David's, Topeka, Kansas, is in 'real' America, the deepest Mid-West, where one expects to find small-town values and apple-pie order. And so one does, except for the fact that Topeka harbours an independent religious group, which, like similar ecclesiastical organizations, believes the Bible is capable of black and white literal interpretation. Accordingly the group has simple views on most things. In particular, they consign to eternal damnation that percentage of the population born gay, together with Roman Catholics,

---

21 Gregory Dix, 1964, *The Shape of the Liturgy*, London: A. and C. Black, p. v.

Jews and Muslims, and Americans, Canadians and Swedes for encouraging the aforementioned. The group makes it their solemn business relentlessly to picket churches that are inclusive of gay persons, and do so in a way to cause maximum hurt and offence. On the night St David's community lost its building to an arsonist, the group was on hand with placards that read 'Burn, baby, burn!' You get the general picture.

For many years, the community of St David's has been subjected to such abuse Sunday after Sunday, and has borne it with dignified silence. Tough though it is, this experience means that the leaders of the children's education programme in the parish never have to search for a means of bringing alive the early church to the kids; here the early church has come to them. No longer merely the stuff of history books, the early Christian experience of persecution is being re-enacted every time they meet; with the kids themselves playing a leading role.

Gathering for formation

Because we gather with other human beings, in communities in which by definition all the saints are sinners, gathering can never be all sweetness and light. There are one or two people we may wish to avoid as well as the majority we wish to embrace; people we find it difficult to warm to, others we have found it dangerously easy to be too warm to. As in any group of humanity, things have happened and things have been said that stick in our memory, cause us embarrassment, or break our hearts. Gathering therefore is no pushover; it can be costly, uncertain, full of apprehension. But gathering will always be formative; it is a process that knocks us into shape, and smoothes our protruding edges. This will, however, require of us on occasions immense self-control, even courage. To gather alongside those ranged against us on some issue that threatens to divide the church is a stomach-churning business. We shall be awake long before it is time to get up. But it must be done. On the simple act of gathering in these circumstances depends the future of the church.

The instinct to withdraw, to pull away, to secede, to go into schism (while always, of course, claiming to be 'the true church') is a tragic falling away from the path that Christ trod on his lonely and fearful journey to Jerusalem, a path to which we are also called. The instinct to scatter, rather than gather, is one born of spiritual arrogance and leads inevitably to disintegration. In taking our bat home, we place our own preferences or prejudices before the common good, our pursuit of that elusive goal 'truth' before the primary goal demanded by our Teacher, which is love. Jesus speaks of his own ministry as one that demands a response in which gathering is but one of two available options: 'Whoever is not with me is against me, and whoever does not gather with me scatters' (Matthew 12.30).

Gathering for proclamation

More often, however, the Christian scriptures speak of gathering as bound up with a final reckoning at the end time, when all is brought together and consigned either into the domain of God or onto the fire (Matthew 13.30). John the Baptist acclaims Jesus as he who will call the world to account: 'with a winnowing fork in hand, he will clear his threshing floor and gather his wheat into the granary' (Matthew 3.12). Jesus himself teaches us a picture of God who gathers, but in a process in which judgement is at work as well as mercy. When Jesus weeps over Jerusalem, he also reminds the city that it has missed its chance: 'Would that even today you knew the things that make for peace! But now they are hid from your eyes' (Luke 19.41). Moreover, Jesus instructed his followers, when they came across a town or household that would neither receive nor hear them, to 'shake off the dust that is on your feet for a testimony against them' (Mark 6.11). In this sense, gathering too can be an act of prophetic judgement over and against our culture, or against a prevailing sub-culture with power and influence. At a deep level, the very process of gathering for the liturgy, to surrender ourselves to God in worship, offering ourselves as a living sacrifice of praise and thanksgiving, is an affront to 'the culture of the individual'. And because gathering for worship is an experience of waiting on God, it is an affront to the prevailing culture of instant gratification, fast food and 'drive thru' pharmacies. Gathering deliberately slows down the pace of life: we enter a different time zone. We grow more attentive to the things of the Spirit, to lasting values, to the eternal.

Gathering is therefore not just a response to danger, a means of gaining security and solidarity midst adversity. Gathering can contain a challenge to society, provoking those around us to take note, ponder and think again.

Consequences of gathering

In the renewal of eucharistic liturgy today, the revitalization of the experience of gathering is an essential first step. From this the renewal of all the other components of worship will follow. There will be certain architectural and spatial, as well as liturgical, consequences if we mean business.

Architecture and interior design

As I see it, everything about our building, the place where the assembly gathers, should be geared to the primary function of gathering, for only from gathering will all the other functions of our common life follow.[22]

The building should both proclaim gathering, by its appearance and relationship to the street, and facilitate it, by its internal arrangement. If we inherit a traditional building rather than a tailor-made one, this just means that we have to work that little bit harder.

Exterior

The exterior of the church building should encourage gathering by being a building that is attractive in every aspect, a building that prompts you to enter, that

---

22 Issues of the detailed design of the place of gathering are discussed at greater length in Richard Giles, 2004, *Re-pitching the Tent: The Definitive Guide to Reordering Church Buildings for Worship and Mission*, Norwich: Canterbury Press, third edition, pp. 161–6.

embraces you and makes you think that gathering there would not be such a bad idea.

In relation to the street, all visual barriers should be removed, so that the pavement of the street melts into the forecourt of the building without let or hindrance, so that, before you know it, you find yourself at the door. Anything that puts a distance between the passer-by and the doorway, that heightens the sense of exposure or self-consciousness as you cross the 'no man's land' between pavement and entrance, should be avoided.

Care and attention (and financial allocation) should be given to access – how the main doorway is reached with minimum inconvenience for both the disabled and the able-bodied. Ramps for wheelchair access need to be carefully designed to avoid the impression of ramparts and walls that restrict access rather than ease it. The main entrance should be clearly indicated. Everything about the forecourt and approach should cry out 'Come on in!'

The doorway itself should be glazed so as to provide a glimpse of an attractive and welcoming interior, and should be extremely well lit. Even at night, when the building is closed, the gathering space within should have at least minimal lighting left on, to leave a lasting impression of warmth and welcome to the passer by. After all, what they glimpse through the door is 'home' for a family.

Interior

First, we need to enter together the place of gathering through one channel of assembling, which means saying goodbye to a building with several entrances through which we can slip in and out unnoticed.

Second, this single channel of gathering will lead into a place, a room, an entrance hall, a narthex, which gives clear expression to the common life that we celebrate when we come together.

This means that the place of gathering will rival the liturgical space proper in demanding our attention and causing us to want to linger. It will be generously proportioned, and finely detailed with good hard-wearing materials of high quality. Ongoing maintenance should be of the highest standard also; a dowdy narthex spells a dispirited community. So the lighting will be cosy and welcoming, not harsh and utilitarian (or feeble and dim).

Where we are saddled with an existing building with a small porch as an apology for a narthex, means must be found of creating a gathering place from the space available. In some cases, we shall be able to re-think the whole complex of buildings and transform a church hall into a gathering place from which the worship space is accessed. In other situations, we shall be able to insert into an existing nave a gathering place that is both spacious and elegant.

Whatever the means of our creating a gathering place, the end product will first and foremost be a place of hospitality. It will be a reassuring place where we can take our breath, find the loo and dust ourselves down. From the gathering place it should be possible to look into the liturgical space without feeling propelled into it – we can take our time.

In the gathering space there will be giant notice boards

exhibiting the life of the faith community and its concerns, with lots of (up-to-date!) photographs of key members whom you may wish to identify, as well as of social functions, social action in the neighbourhood and links to third world countries. All this will give a snapshot of the kind of people we are in this community, and will speak volumes even when there is no one present to explain further.

Whenever the building is in use, a rota of members of the faith community should ensure that the welcome is personal, and provide information as well as being a signposting service to other caring agencies in the locality.

On Sundays and other days when the community gathers for worship, the gathering space should include tables spread with cloths, with flowers and some food already laid out in readiness for later. And perhaps there will be balloons and streamers for special occasions, occasional banners saying 'welcome', or 'congratulations', or 'thank you', a whole host of signs and indicators that a real community inhabits this space and that your presence is valued and makes a difference.

Liturgy

The theme of gathering should be made much of throughout the whole eucharistic liturgy. At the greeting of the people at the beginning of the eucharist, the presider should emphasize the significance of the gathered assembly, its variety, inclusiveness and special character as the people of God called into community and service.

Theologically, gathering is not something we do when

we feel we have a spare Sunday morning, it is an initiative of God who calls us 'out of darkness into the marvellous light of God' (1 Peter 2.9). To be gathered by God to make eucharist is a privilege of incredible significance and joy. It is the role of the presider to recall the assembly at the beginning of every liturgy to this privilege of being gathered by a gracious and forgiving and healing God.

The liturgical action should be so designed as to emphasize at various points the gathering of the assembly around the liturgical foci of the space. Not only at the beginning, but later as the assembly moves to gather around the font, there to recall its first love for God, and then to gather around the ambo to feast on the scriptures, and then around the altar-table to taste and see how gracious the Lord is, it is reminded forcibly of its calling to be a pilgrim people, travelling light, remembering that 'here we have no lasting city, but we are looking for the city that is to come' (Hebrews 13.14).

At each of these pivotal points in the liturgy, the presider can call upon the assembly to realize its identity and its potential as the gathered community of God's faithful. If the assembly remains static, on the other hand, its ability to seize hold of this basic theological concept of journey will remain an elusive goal, for there will be a chasm of disconnection between the preached theory and the actual experience of worship.

A lively meaningful liturgy is one in which gathering is not just an introductory theme, but a repeated motif. Gathering is the event by which we, the scattered people of God, are brought back by God's grace into a renewed relationship of reconciliation and peace, with God and with each other. Furthermore, once gathered, we are shown by scripture and by the present, living Christ Jesus, our potential in him as a people of transforming power.

But it all begins with gathering. Once we are assembled, we can set off. The journey of our liturgy, and of our Spirit-filled life, can begin.

Word

NICOLA SLEE

Word, speaking

Liturgy assumes a prior address from the one who, from before time, has called us into being, made us in the divine image and looks for our response of love. We leave our beds and homes, we meet together, we gather around the eucharistic table, we offer intercession and thanksgiving – all in response to a sense, however dim, of being drawn by one who knew and loved us long before we reached out in reply. We seek the living word that speaks into our hearts and our lives because that word has already spoken, has already taken the initiative, is already addressing and forming us; and will go on doing so all the days of our lives.

In both Christian and Jewish tradition, the word is so much more than a verbal or written word, even the honoured words of scripture – though, of course, scripture is one of the key places where Christians and Jews look to find echoes, intimations and interpretations of that word. The word, *dabhar* in Hebrew, is the living, active, dynamic presence of God, spoken in creation as well as in the revelation of Christ, which has been with God from the beginning and without whom nothing that is exists (John 1.1–3). In the wisdom literature, the word is imaged as Lady Sophia, the one who was with God from the beginning (Proverbs 8.22–31), who played with God from before the dawn of time, who calls continually to human beings to come to her banquet, to drink of her wine, to imbibe of her wisdom (Proverbs 8.1–4; 9.1–5). This word or wisdom is the source of all knowledge and truth – not abstract, intellectual knowledge, but the wisdom that leads to right living, to the conduct of justice and peace in communal, as well as personal life. God longs to pour out this wisdom upon all people, and indeed has done so and continues to do so. It is of the very being of God to give, to pour out God's very life for the world, to self-offer; and this is what we mean by speaking of the word that is uttered from God's mouth. It is a powerful metaphor of the way in which God continually pours out God's very life-breath, God's very being and meaning, to the world.

Ultimately, the word for Christians is Jesus Christ, the beloved, who comes to us in flesh and blood as the manifestation of God's truth: a human being who shows us what it means to live God's truth and seek God's way; a word-in-action, a word translated into terms we can handle, touch, hear and see (1 John 1.1–3) – not, in the first place, therefore, a text, a doctrine or a concept, but a life, a life that engaged all the realities of our human lives (pain, desire, hunger, thirst, glory, suffering) and revealed God in the midst of them. But the word is not exhausted even by the life and death of Jesus of

Nazareth, normative as these are for Christians. The word as Christ is the risen and exalted one, present by faith within the Christian community and within the whole created world as the Spirit released and set free to blow where the Spirit wills: and therefore able to speak in and through many guises and voices, not only recognizably Christian ones – coming to God's people through all forms of creativity and artistry, scholarly and practical wisdom, and in all genuine striving after truth and justice. God's word will not be contained by any of the limits Christians may set to impose upon it, but will speak where God will.

I have wanted to paint the broadest possible canvas as the setting for considering 'the liturgy of the word' within the wider eucharistic liturgy because I believe that, unless we do, we are very likely to narrow down and domesticate our understanding of the ways in which God speaks to us. We are liable to make God's word into *our* words, to reduce the living word to a holy text, to limit the freedom, sovereignty and graciousness of God's ever-seeking wisdom to *our* particular concerns and favoured concepts. The word that we seek to hear, engage and respond to in the eucharist is the word that has uttered forth the whole world and continues to speak throughout the world, in all its glory and brokenness. Our liturgical gatherings are times and spaces in which we seek to receive and respond to that word with particular attention, in the company of others seeking the same thing, but only so that we can be more alive to hearing God's word in the liturgy of our whole lives and in the life of the world.

If 'the word' cannot be limited to Bible, church texts or doctrines, or even to the human life and death of Jesus of Nazareth, then equally the 'ministry of the word' within the eucharistic liturgy cannot be limited to that particular section of the liturgy, though we may focus particular attention upon listening to the word in that part of the liturgy we describe as such. We might think of the whole of the eucharistic liturgy as the space in which God speaks to us, uttering the life-giving word. We receive this word in eating and drinking at the table as much as we do in breaking open the scriptures and giving voice to our own prayers and concerns.[23] As Ruben Alves has arrestingly suggested, we are dealing with a word that is 'good enough to eat'![24]

Hearing the word

Given that God has spoken, is speaking, and will for ever utter the word, the first task and duty of those engaged in public worship is simply to listen. This is the heart of all liturgy, as it is the heart of all prayer. All the words, actions, gestures and work we bring to liturgy are only of value in so far as they enable us to attune our hearts and beings to *listen* to and *hear* what the Spirit is saying. 'Let

23 Stephen Burns, in 2006, *Liturgy* (SCM Studyguide), London: SCM Press, pp.31–2, points to the ways in which there is an interplay between word and sacrament in the eucharist, with the sense of the word as sacramental echoed by the sense of the sacraments as 'visible words'.

24 Ruben Alves, 1988, *The Poet, The Warrior and the Prophet*, London: SCM Press.

anyone with ears listen', Jesus says (Matthew 11.13 et al.; and see Revelation 2.7, 11, 17 et al.).

Hearing the word, really hearing it with our whole being, is something both utterly simple and extremely hard. It is both gift and labour: something we have to work at, both collectively and individually; and something that we do not deserve or earn but is graciously given to us out of God's abundance. Our part is to do all that we can to make space for the word to be spoken, to cultivate the habits and disciplines that will allow the word to be heard: it is up to God, in God's freedom, to speak as and when God wills.

There are all kinds of barriers and hindrances that get in the way of us hearing the word. Some of these barriers are internal, concerned with our own inner dispositions, learned habits, attitudes and psychological hang-ups; others are external, created by the social, cultural and religious context in which we find ourselves – and, of course, inner and outer are intimately interconnected. We need to pay attention to both sorts of barriers when we are considering the work that has to be done to clear the ground and open up a space for God's word to be planted, take root and grow.

Starting with the second of these – the outer, it is essential that we acknowledge and really wrestle with the fact that God's word is spoken within the context, terms and condition of our human communities, cultures and traditions – which means, at the very least, that we have no access to that word in any kind of objective, pure, unsullied form (though some Christians seem to think so). Whether we are talking about the Bible, the life and death of Jesus of Nazareth or God's word in creation, God speaks and self-reveals in all the ambiguity, complexity and messiness of the real world in which biblical texts came to be written and transmitted, in which Jesus lived out his own life, in which creation groans and labours towards the freedom to which it aspires (Romans 8.22–23). In each case, there is no straightforward access to some transcendent, unchanging word that drops, like parcels from an aeroplane, from the sky.

Part of what it means to believe in incarnation is that God's communication is always within the messiness, even the sinfulness, of human lives and contexts. So, for example, with reference to the Bible, the word is spoken in and through very human texts – which means, as any reader of the Bible knows, that we have to work hard to hear a word in and through exploits of wars, turmoil, kinship squabbles, brutish violence or through laws about ritual purity and minutiae of food preparation that seem to have very little relevance to our lives. As a female reader of the Bible, I frequently feel alienated from a text that largely ignores women and, when it does acknowledge our existence, often treats us as second-class citizens. Black readers, gay and lesbian readers or blind readers, among others, may all regard the Bible with similar suspicion. Elizabeth Schüssler Fiorenza has suggested that the Bible ought to carry a health warning: 'Can be dangerous to your health.'[25] There are good

25 Quoted by Ann Loades, 1987, *Searching for Lost Coins: Explorations in Christianity and Feminism*, London: SPCK, p. 5.

reasons why Anglicans have never made an absolute identification between the Bible and the word of God, recognizing rather that the Bible testifies to the word, the Bible can become, in the work of the Spirit, the word God speaks to us – but not without a great deal of help from the tradition (which, of course, itself is equally ambivalent, marked by histories of colonialism, patriarchy, militarism, and so on), from our own experience and from contemporary interpreters.

These external problems are very real barriers to hearing the word of God, and the Christian church needs to take them very seriously – as liberation, feminist, postcolonial, gay, lesbian, queer and disabled theologians, among others, are doing, though their insights seem hardly to reach many pulpits or congregations! Allied to these external factors, there are also the internal ones that prevent us hearing a living word: our own obsessive preoccupations with ourselves; our very real hurts, wounds and pains – whether self-inflicted or inflicted by others – that can make it difficult for us even to believe there might be a word of salvation uttered to our situation, let alone to receive it; our manically over-busy lives and minds, constantly distracted by relentless pressures, noise and the materialism of our culture, which promises to offer us all that our insatiable greed, massaged by the messages of that culture, has been taught to desire.

Yet, to repeat: to believe in incarnation is to believe that God speaks precisely in and through the conditions and the contexts in which we find ourselves, in which the church is placed in the world. So, while we must recognize and wrestle with these barriers and obstructions, yet we must also look hopefully to the word that is spoken, not apart from, but absolutely within the messiness, contradictions and distractions of our lives.

I would like to suggest a range of disciplines and habits that might help us, in the liturgy, to clear the space for God's word to be heard; remembering always that God's word ultimately is God's gift, which cannot be dictated or controlled by anything we say or do – but recognizing that we have a responsibility to do all that we can to clear the space in which such a word can be uttered. First, and most obviously, it is important that the words that are spoken within the liturgy, and particularly the spoken words of scripture, are clearly and imaginatively conveyed, with proper attention to the context and needs of the hearers. Scripture should be read well, and this requires proper training, so that people are enabled to do it to the very best of their different abilities; many people in our day are not accustomed to reading aloud and so need encouragement to do it well, and, even as they get better at it, much of scripture will be alien and difficult to the hearers. It can be helpful for members of the congregation to have the text of the readings printed out on screen or paper, or to have copies of the Bible to hand (and it's good to have a range of translations available). Inclusive language translations should always be preferred. Some contemporary versions of the Bible, such as *The Message*,[26] *The Street Bible*[27] or, less well known,

---

26 Eugene Peterson, 1994, *The Message*, Colorado Springs, CO: NavPress.

27 Rob Lacey, 2002, *The Street Bible*, Grand Rapids, MI: Zondervan.

the *Good as New* version of the New Testament,[28] can really bring the text alive to contemporary congregations unfamiliar with the biblical world.[29] There are many different ways of reading – or perhaps better, *performing* – the text of scripture. Dramatic readings of narratives, using different voices and/or groups within the congregation; responsorial readings of psalms and canticles; sung or chanted portions of scripture – these are all different ways of bringing the word off the page and making it live within the gathered assembly.

Second, the word needs to be heard with and within the whole body, both corporate and individual. We are apt to think of the word as something we hear only with the outer ear and inner mind or intellect; but if, as I have stressed throughout, the word is so much more than mere text or speech-event, then, too, we hear it with so much more than the ear or the mind. Anyone who has ever been to a live concert, whether of classical music, folk or rock, knows that music is felt as much as heard, as vibrations in the belly and all up and down one's arms and legs.[30] We hear with our whole bodies, which is

28 John Hensen, 2004, *Good as New: A Radical Retelling of the Scriptures*, Ropley: O Books.

29 For public reading of the bible, Gordon W. Lathrop and Gail Ramshaw, eds, 1995–7, *Readings for the Assembly*, Volumes 1, 2 and 3, Minneapolis, MN: Augsburg Fortress Press, is an especially notable resource, in that it offers a lectionary based on the New Revised Standard Version of the Bible in which sexist language has been minimized and inclusive language artfully and unobtrusively employed throughout. The three volumes correspond to the three-year cycle of the Revised Common Lectionary.

30 A fantastic exploration of the way in which sound is heard

perhaps one good reason why in some traditions it is customary to stand for the Gospel reading – not only out of respect, but also as a way of indicating with our whole bodies: 'we are alert, we are ready, we are standing on tiptoe of expectation to hear what you are saying to us, O Christ!' So how we place our bodies in liturgy – how and where we sit, how we are placed in relation to the lectern, how we are placed in relation to *each other*, what we look at, when we stand and sit down, the various postures we adopt: all these are important for creating within the body of Christ the conditions in which we can hear the word God wants to speak to us. If, for example, the seating is in serried rows all facing the altar or the pulpit, we pick up a fairly obvious, if subliminal, message about where the source of authority lies, where we are most likely to hear the word (in the sacrament or sermon, respectively) and from whom (priest or preacher) – and where we are least likely to hear it (from each other, the ones we are sitting next to, for example).

If we hear with our whole body, this includes our eyes and our entire senses (cf. 1 John 1.1). And indeed, many of our churches testify to the fact that the word is spoken in and through the visual, the tactile and the aural. Think of all the artistry, dedication and labour – not to mention money – expended on stained-glass windows, murals and friezes, sculptures, wood carvings, textile and needlecraft, and of course the glorious traditions of church

---

with the whole body is *Touching the Sound*, a documentary about the profoundly deaf percussionist, Evelyn Glennie.

music. Despite the Reformation, the Anglican Church has never wholly turned its back on the arts. Its finest buildings, as well as some of its simplest, testify to the way in which God utters the word through shape and colour, texture and line, sound and movement. In our own time, the visual in particular is being reclaimed as perhaps *the* primary medium, and many churches do make use of PowerPoint, banner or OHP – though often in a narrowly functional way, as a means of communicating information (words of hymns or choruses, for example) rather than in a more imaginative way to stimulate sense and imagination. But there is huge scope for rendering the word in image and sound: as one example only, it is easy to raid the worldwide web to find images of biblical texts and narratives, and these can be converted into PowerPoint to accompany the reading of the biblical text (with due regard for copyright).

Third, we need to take with radical seriousness the fact that God speaks in a multiplicity of languages and cultures. Even if the particular congregation in which we are rooted is not as various as those in most cosmopolitan cities, the world in which we live *is* gloriously and beautifully multiple – and our liturgies ought to reflect that, in ways that are appropriate, sensitive and context-specific, to be sure. God's word is never monotone nor mono-cultural. God is not, as some still seem inclined to think, a well-bred, well-spoken Englishman! We need to let the word break out of the cultural prisons in which we often seek, knowingly or unconsciously, to contain it; let it speak in many tongues and in the forms of many cultures. Perhaps the place to start is by paying attention to the constituency of our own congregations and wider communities. Even the most remote rural villages are more diverse than we often imagine, and people's families are rarely monochrome. Once we start paying attention to the people that make up the living body of Christ, we discover many varied histories and geographies that make up the tapestry of the local community. These can be honoured and reflected in all kinds of ways, from the most simple to the highly ambitious. In my own parish, for example – a fairly fluid city congregation with people from many ethnic, class and national backgrounds, not all of whom speak much English – people are always invited to say the Prayer That Jesus Taught (cf. Matthew 6.9–13) 'in your mother-tongue or in the language most comfortable to you'. Hymns, songs and chants from the world church, in a variety of languages, are regularly sung within the liturgy. Sometimes, a scripture reading will be read in more than one language.

And when we think about language and culture, we need to go beyond nationality and ethnicity, paying attention to language and discourse in the widest possible sense. Is the liturgy routinely couched in the cultural forms and discourse of the educated middle classes, for example? Asking this question has all kinds of implications, ranging from how text-based our liturgy is (many cultures operate in a primarily aural medium) to thinking about the kinds of people – and voices – that routinely address the congregation from lectern or prayer-desk (are they all white, English, over 50?). Whose voices do we hear speaking God's word and do they represent the full range of voices through which God can and longs to speak? In Anglican liturgy, the readings from scripture are one of the key places where lay people regularly have a voice and particular visibility, and, precisely because they are in a representative role, expressing the participation of the whole *laos*, it is important that, over time, those fulfilling this role really do represent the full range of people within the community.

Finally, if we are to put ourselves in the place where we can hear and attend to the word, then the liturgy needs to cultivate a genuine collective listening: not only at set times when scripture is read or the sermon is delivered, but throughout the entire act of worship. Liturgy needs to be conducted within a context of attentive and alert expectation; each person coming to prayer needs to be encouraged to come with an expectation of being addressed, and the gathered assembly as a whole needs to meet in this expectation. There are widely differing customs surrounding silence in liturgy, but whatever the cultural setting and mores, silence has a crucial role to play in the enabling of the congregation to hear the word. The liturgy, when it is a living, dynamic event, has its own internal rhythm of address and response, of speaking and listening, of speech and silence, of gesture and stillness. The word has its roots in the silence of God[31] and silence is a requisite for hearing that word –

31 As is expressed in the beautiful Wisdom text, used as the Magnificat antiphon at Christmastide: 'When peaceful silence lay over all, and night was in the midst of her swift course, from your royal throne O God, down from the heavens, leapt your almighty Word.' See 2005, *Common Worship: Daily Prayer*, London: Church House Publishing, p. 223.

whether that silence is held before the liturgy as people gather, or in the spaces between different parts of the liturgy: after scripture readings, after the sermon, within the intercessions, at the end of the eucharistic prayer. As Sister Jeremy Hall says, writing about the significance of silence within the life of prayer, silence is not an end in itself, but 'it is for the word – to hear the word with the ear of the heart, to let it enter deeply and fully, and then to speak out of that depth in loving response'.[32]

Engaging the word

As we begin to hear the word, and really pay attention to it, we are already beginning to engage with it – and it with us. For to listen, to attend, to really hear, is never a purely passive act (although receptivity is a key aspect of it) but is a response of involvement, an active offering of the mind, heart, body and will *to* the word, to be worked on by the word – to be sifted, plumbed, nurtured, fed and converted.

So we should not make any kind of artificial distinction between the act of hearing the word and the process of engaging it within the liturgy. Nevertheless, there is a kind of rhythm or movement from one to the other within the liturgy. The liturgy of the word begins by the proclamation of the word in scripture and the work of the congregation at this point is primarily one of listening – albeit with the eye, the body, the senses and not

32 Jeremy Hall, 2007, *Silence, Solitude, Simplicity: A Hermit's Love Affair with a Noisy, Crowded, and Complicated World*, Collegeville, MN: Liturgical Press, p. 26.

only the ear. Then the word is taken up – usually in preaching, although preaching is only one form of doing so – and broken open for the particular community present at the liturgy. Now the task becomes more than listening and hearing: we are required actively to engage, to reflect, to ponder, to wrestle with the word, to interpret what that word is saying to our particular time, lives, needs, crises and opportunities. This is the point in the liturgy where we pay very explicit attention to the twofold dialogue between the word of God spoken in scripture, creation and revelation, and the context of the world in which we live here and now, in our own particular country, community and networks, and seek to bring the two 'horizons' together.

Traditionally, the work of interpreting the word, and of applying it to hearers' context has been done through the medium of the sermon, where one trained in biblical scholarship and theology and sensitive to the needs and condition of the contemporary world wrestles with the set scripture readings and seeks to discern a particular word for the people. Preaching has an honoured place in Anglican tradition, and the best preaching continues to have a capacity to engage and enliven mind, heart and will, and to provoke the kind of internal (and sometimes external) dialogue that the ministry of the word is intended to engage. Good preaching will stimulate hearers into active listening, questioning, pondering and discovery, so that each person herself or himself becomes involved in that two-way conversation between God's revelation in scripture, Christ and creation, on the one hand, and the contemporary setting, on the other.

But the sermon is not the only means of engaging the word, and there are particular reasons why, in our day, the sermon may not be the best – or certainly not the *only* – means of engaging congregations. In a media-saturated world, many people have un-learned the skill (or never acquired it) of listening to one person speaking, without interruption, for more than five minutes or so. In a world where the majority of communication is now visual rather than primarily aural, and where television and computer reign over the book, many are unaccustomed to being addressed exclusively through the medium of the spoken word. Moreover, in a world where there is a general – and necessary – suspicion of institutional authority, where many groups of people (women, black, gay and lesbian persons and so on) have become conscious of the ways in which power has been used against them and their own right to speak denied, the sermon can all too readily be associated with, and be experienced as, dominating, top-down, un-negotiated power exercised by one mandated individual over others. None of this necessarily spells the death of the sermon (though some think so), but at the very least, it does require preachers to be acutely sensitive to all the reasons why it is hard for people to listen to and engage with the preached word. And it invites the imaginative employment of other means than the sermon for engaging the word.[33]

There are, of course, all kinds of sermon, and many

33 *Common Worship* recognizes this in its rubric on The Sermon: 'The sermon may on occasion include less formal exposition of Scripture, the use of drama, interviews, discussion and audio-visual aids' (p. 332).

different ways of preaching. Many preachers prefer to speak from a lectern on the same level as the congregation rather than to enter the pulpit and be lifted 'six feet above contradiction'; some preachers will actively involve members of the congregation in question and answer dialogue (although this can, in its own way, be as coercive as a monologue); sermons can make use of visual illustration, and draw imaginatively on many sources – from video clips to extracts of music – to move beyond the use of words alone. Dialogue sermons where two preachers converse together about the scriptural texts, are an alternative to solo preaching, or the whole congregation can be actively engaged in discussing the texts. For a number of years I belonged to the St Hilda Community in London, where the common practice was for those gathered to break up into small groups of four or five to discuss the readings. This was a way of giving recognition to each person's lived experience and bringing it to bear on the biblical text, a way of calling each person to the task of interpreting and applying the scriptures to their lives. A prolonged period of silence might be kept after the readings, in which the dialogue of interpretation and engaging takes place internally, in the mind and heart of each person, rather than externally – and perhaps then a space given for people to share brief comments afterwards. Or a particular group within a congregation – such as the youth group or a study group – might be given the task of reflecting on the readings and bringing a short presentation to the wider congregation.[34]

---

34 See Stephen Burns' discussion of the sermon for further ideas, *Liturgy* (SCM Studyguide), pp. 88–90.

Whatever particular methods of interpreting and engaging the word are used, there are certain principles that apply. All that I have said above about listening in and with the entire body applies to our attempts to engage with the word through sermon, reflection, meditation or other means: the imagination and whole physical selves of the participants need to be engaged in the interpretation of the word, since this word is addressed to our whole lives, not simply our minds. At the same time, those who help to interpret and apply the word do need to engage the mind and the brain of their listeners. The sermon is not a lecture, and the liturgical assembly is not a lecture hall, but God has given us minds with which to think and we are intended to use them in wrestling with scripture. Preachers have a particular responsibility to study the work of biblical scholars and others whose knowledge and insight can help to break open the scriptures in helpful and meaningful ways. And just as we should expect an intelligent application to the study of God's word in scripture by those who seek to interpret it to us, so we should expect an intelligent and committed study of God's word in the world from those who preach and teach. If the sermon (in whatever form) is truly to engage the dialogue between scripture and contemporary world, then we need preachers who know God's world well and deeply, who are able to draw on the full range of human knowledge, culture and expertise to interpret God's word. Exactly how and to what extent the work of scholars, contemporary commentators, artists, scientists and so on, is drawn on within the sermon will depend enormously on the particular skills of the preacher and on the culture of the congregation. Whatever the level of education of preacher or congregation, however, there are many ways of being thoughtful, intelligent and intellectually engaged.

Part of what this means is to be honest and authentic in one's engagement with the word – and this is a core principle in any form of preaching or interpretation of the scriptures. I want and need preachers[35] to be honest about what they find difficult, alien or offensive in scripture – for if they are not honest, how can I be truthful about my own struggles? If a text is frankly misogynist or exults in a violent, militarist God, the preacher needs to say so and help the congregation wrestle with how they are to hear a liberating word in and through such a text. I want and need preachers to be honest about the church's very chequered history of militarism, patriarchy, slavery and so on. I want and need preachers to wrestle with the difficult questions that life poses to faith: questions of unjust suffering, abuse of the innocent, the instability of the physical universe that leads to natural disasters. I want and need preachers to bring the text to bear on the real issues of people's lives that have often been ignored or denied in the pulpit: the struggles and delights of family life, for example (including different forms of family groupings, sexual and other forms of

35 I am using the term 'preacher' here and throughout as a shorthand for any person or persons who interpret the word in the context of the liturgy, whether through the medium of a traditional sermon or not. Similarly, when I speak of 'sermon', I have in mind the broad range of different possible methods of communication mentioned.

violence within the home and so on), as well as the struggles and achievements that people face daily in their working lives, in business, commerce, politics, the law, education, health care and so on.

Commitment to diversity and inclusion is another principle that applies to the preaching and interpretation of scripture. Since scripture itself is so pervasively patriarchal (with some scholars estimating that women appear in only about one tenth of the text), preachers need to be intentional about making women and women's lives fully present in the sermon (it's still very common to hear sermons that make not a single reference to women). Since Christian tradition has been, until very recently, so pervasively Eurocentric and racist, then again, preachers need consciously to think about how to stand against that tradition and proclaim the word in ways that embrace all. The preacher needs to work to ensure that the word can be heard by all present, and that means taking with utmost seriousness the particularities of context and life experience of those present.

Responding to the word

Having heard and engaged with the word through listening to the scriptures and interpreting and applying them to our own specific situation through sermon or some other means, the liturgy moves on to the collective response of the congregation to God's word. This collective response takes two forms: first, the recitation of the Creed, and, next, the offering of intercessory prayer. In the proclamation of the Creed, we make a response of belief, of assent to God who is creator, saviour and sustainer of the world, by joining in some form of the church's confession of faith. In the offering of prayer, we make a response of love and care for God's world, a commitment of a different kind – offering our passion and compassion for those in particular need, and for those for whom we have a duty of care. Both forms of commitment are important, and mutually reinforce each other. Making a commitment of belief alone is a mere cerebral act unless that belief is worked out in our prayer and our action. But that prayer and service itself needs to be rooted in a wider, collective confession of faith if it is to be sustained. Without prayer and the action that springs from prayer, belief is likely to be moribund. Without theology, study and intellectual assent, spirituality and action are likely to be unreflective and superficial.

For many contemporary churchgoers, the saying of the Creed may represent one of the more perplexing and alienating aspects of the liturgy. Perhaps even more than scripture, the Creeds are couched in language and thought forms from a remote thought world, and few lay Christians have much, if any, understanding of the particular historical and philosophical contexts out of which they took form. In recognition of this, most of the churches offer alternative versions of the Creed; *Common Worship* has seven authorized affirmations of faith, for example, in addition to the Nicene, Apostles' and Athanasian Creeds.[36] Not that any of these versions offer

36 *Common Worship*, pp. 138–48.

straightforward affirmations of faith; and each of them requires its own interpretation if people are going to be enabled to join in the words intelligently, with conviction and understanding. Even so, in the collective confession of faith within the liturgy, the emphasis is far less on individuals' right belief (as if this were some kind of 'test' of belief we each have to pass in order to gain the right to be part of worship!) than on the allegiance to the tradition of faith to which we, as individuals and congregations, belong. It is significant that most of the classic creeds (though not the Apostles') use the collective pronoun 'We' rather than the individual 'I'. In confessing our shared faith, we align ourselves to that great cloud of witnesses who have confessed faith in Christ throughout the ages, and join ourselves to their witness. We are part of that tradition by virtue of our shared baptism and participation in Christ, whether or not we hold exactly the same beliefs or understanding of those beliefs as those who have come before us (which, in point of fact, we almost certainly do not and cannot do). As I write, there has been some debate, in the letters page of *The Church Times*, about the extent to which Anglicans are bound by the doctrines of the Thirty-Nine Articles, the Book of Common Prayer and the Ordinal, and what allegiance to such classic authorities means. I find myself in concurrence with Jonathan Clatworthy, who robustly refutes the idea that we can believe exactly the same as Thomas Cranmer ('Cranmer himself would be the last to expect it') and goes on: 'Contrary to much popular rhetoric, there is no virtue in believing what our predecessors believed just because they believed it. What does have virtue is the commitment to seek the truth, wherever it leads us; and to do so is to follow in the footsteps of Cranmer at his best.'[37] So we can, in good conscience, join in the words of the Creeds even as we struggle to understand them, rail against their patriarchal and pre-scientific language, or doubt the strength of our own personal convictions or orthodoxy. Christians have always argued, struggled and disagreed about the boundaries of right belief, and the discussion is ongoing. Many would argue that the classic Creeds provide a framework of belief that still allows a great deal of room for debate, even while they clearly reflect the preoccupations of their own time. In joining in the words of the Creed, we are committing ourselves as much to the ongoing work of theological study and reflection that the Creeds themselves embody and that has always been part of the life of the church, as we are to any one, limited interpretation of faith.

Responding in collective, intercessory prayer to God's word spoken in scripture and sermon is a way of taking very seriously the claim of the word on our lives, and seeking to put it into action. It is part of the ongoing rhythm of receiving and giving, of listening and addressing that forms the heart-beat of the liturgy. As we have heard a word that challenges, convicts, comforts or chastens us, so we bring ourselves back to God in prayer, asking for God's help in applying the word to our lives. And we bring not only ourselves, but all those to whom we are in some way connected by threads of kinship,

37 Letters page of *The Church Times*, 1 February 2008.

culture, locality or concern, recognizing that the word God has spoken is not only for us – the ones who happen to be gathered in this particular congregation and church – but for the wider communities of which we are a part. So we pray – for church, world, neighbourhood, those who suffer, the departed and ourselves. In praying, we bring before God symbolically the life of the world, giving thanks for its goodness and beauty and seeking help for its brokenness and suffering. It is one of the chief places in the liturgy where we very explicitly face outwards, beyond the walls of our immediate gathering, anticipating the end of the liturgy when we will leave church and go out 'to live and work to God's praise and glory', seeking to serve those we meet and live alongside.

Alongside the reading of scripture, the leading of intercessions is a key place within the liturgy for lay leadership. As those who live and work within the world – in distinction from clergy who are, typically, set aside from the world to administer the domestic life of the church – the laity by their very presence represent the needs of the world within the assembly, and it is fitting that they should therefore be the ones to voice these needs in the public prayer of the congregation. Just as there are many different ways to preach, so there are many different ways to offer prayer, and our liturgies should reflect the full range. Authorized rites tend to offer suggested frameworks, with many alternatives, but none of these is mandatory, and there is much scope for creativity here. Resources to support the offering of intercession are legion, and there is no earthly reason why the intercessions should be tedious, routine or stale (as they sometimes, sadly, are), given the wide availability of written prayers from around the globe and from every denomination and spiritual tradition. Nor need prayer be offered only in words; all that I have said above about the use of the visual and other media applies here. Symbolic action and gesture can play a meaningful role. The lighting and placing of candles to represent intercessory intentions or thanksgiving is a common practice in many places. Similarly, stones or flowers can be placed, either silently or with spoken intentions. Members of congregations can be invited to write their concerns on pieces of paper, which are gathered up and offered on the altar. Dance and drama can express prayer very powerfully. Silence, too, will have an essential part to play in the time given to prayer. The possibilities are endless, and this is one place in the liturgy where we can encourage each other to pray in a wide variety of ways.

Word enfleshed

As we meet the living word in scripture and sacrament; as we seek to respond faithfully, intelligently and lovingly to that word, we find that the word is formed mysteriously within us. The word enfleshed in Christ is enfleshed in our own bodies and blood, coming to dwell in us. And so, as the gathering of the assembly is dispersed and we go out from worship, we carry this word with us, in our very hearts and mouths, ready to speak it and to give it out in our own lives, mirroring the way that God continually utters and gives the word to the world.

The word we have looked upon, touched and handled with our own hands, is the incarnate word present in our own lives, bodies and blood – and ready to meet us in the enfleshed life of the world, which is itself the body of God.

Table

ANN LOADES

Table: sacramental spirituality

At one level, as we reflect on it, being 'at table' together is nothing out of the ordinary. For human creatures all over the world, in all times and places, readily share food and drink with one another – at least, when there is enough to go round. The offering of hospitality in the sharing of a meal may be especially significant for those who endure insecurity and near-starvation and for that very reason may be generous to strangers. Being 'companions', that is, able to eat 'bread' or whatever is the 'staff of life' in a given culture, is integral not merely to survival, but to flourishing and fulfilment, being gradually transformed into the best sort of person of which we, with others, are capable. It is at meal times especially, giving one another 'face-time', sharing life with one another in convivial ways, that we make a gift of our identities one to another. We may be more or less wordless, lively in speech as well as gesture, expressive of ourselves in 'body language', including what we wear, how we enhance our faces and altogether present ourselves in our shared worlds of meaning. We come to find ourselves in communities as neighbours, as story-tellers, gossips and natterers, jokers, in more or less serious conversations and exchanges of help. At least sometimes we experience *joie de vivre*, real delight and relaxation and trust in one another. We 'toast' one another at meals. And a tiny gesture of courtesy, such as passing a dish of food, is practice for more generous gestures to one another. The same holds true for moments of apology. In these sorts of ways we discover ourselves to be anything but self-made. We are in a sense creatures of one another.

In many unprecedented ways compared with our ancestors, we also may come to appreciate our non-human context, in which we find ourselves to be co-adapted, co-evolved with one another and with non-human beings, who are as much 'at home' here as we are. We relish, for example, Richard Attenborough's revelation to us on film of the creatures that exist for themselves and for God, as well as for our astonishment and delight, and even, with what should be much reverence and caution, sometimes for our use – gifts to us indeed. In other words, we share our inheritance with our human and non-human forebears and the present inhabitants of our world. We have reminders of our kinship with other creatures if we keep pets who come to know us and respond to us, and especially perhaps when we depend upon another animal, such as a 'guide dog' for example. We, in turn, can learn much about caring from our ordinary non-human companions, though even more, of course, from caring for the very young of our own species, or for the vulnerable among us. Thus it is in the sheer extra/ordinariness of our lives that we learn that we do not spring from nowhere, in, of and by ourselves. So we should be 'saying grace' not just for the particular gifts of the table, but for our recognition of ourselves as creatures in relation to all others. Our maxims should include 'only connect' and 'ignore nothing'!

Sacramental spirituality: ignore nothing!

We deem ourselves to be creatures, however, because we learn that creatureliness has a further and even more profound sense, and one that may become a foundation for our understanding even of that prior sense of creaturely-relatedness to all other beings. We do not discover this from scratch, though we have to appropriate it for ourselves. We may come to appreciate that our whole context is that of 'creation', that is, it is derived from and sustained in all its immensity and detail by God. It is God who provides our world with life-giving resources, an endless source of wonder and thankfulness – despite those features that may horrify us. It is not all here just for us, as it were, and it does not suit all of us all the time. Nonetheless, the abundance and variety of our created context is such that whether we simply look around us, find our way about, or explore it by an astonishing variety of means – including major technological achievements such as satellites or telescopes or microscopes – and organize what we find in theory and sign and symbol, we learn that it is truly 'ours'. This is where we share life together and make and re-make our worlds of meaning. But also we trust that the whole cosmic totality is related in the most radical way to God, whom we can neither possess nor control, who – beyond all our attempts – is unnameable, who is sometimes inexplicable, unpredictable and surprising.

Despite our cautious and important realization that God is 'unsayable' and beyond our idolatries, in finding ourselves as creatures we hear, read and sing 'God' in a splendid variety of ways, trying to remember at all times that our language for God has an 'is/but is not' character. And we note in passing that religious believers of many persuasions have the opportunity to learn from one another about what this may mean in ways available to us as never before. This can be both unnerving and invigorating, but it is not to our purpose at the moment to elaborate on this point. Rather we need to try to orientate ourselves by drawing on resources readily available to us. We may draw on ancient texts. 'Heaven and earth are full of thy glory' comes from the awesome praise of God as 'Holy' in Isaiah (Isaiah 6.6) – glory as authoritative, splendid, discernible, as in the *Sanctus* of Christian liturgy.[38] We begin to sing or say 'Glory to God in the highest' and the rest of the *Gloria*.[39] We can look at what artists in paint have done in their portraits of paradise and the harmony there of human and

---

38 The *Sanctus* is the name given to the stanza 'Holy, holy, holy' that, in common with many other traditions, forms part of all the *Common Worship* eucharistic prayers.

39 The *Gloria* 'may be used' in *Common Worship* eucharists (see *Common Worship*, p. 171, where it is the 'default' text, and pp. 330–1, notes 3 and 11).

non-human. We can be illuminated by different renderings of Psalm 104, or chapters 38 and 41 of the Book of Job, William Draper's 'All creatures of our God and King' derived from St Francis of Assisi's 'Canticle of the Creatures',[40] or children singing 'I can sing a rainbow'. Enjoying the many representations of 'Noah's Ark' is not just for the very young! There are so many possibilities both solemn and serious, silly and trivial, on a spectrum from the more or less permanent to the 'throw-away'. In and through it all, we learn 'catholicity', the capacity to attend to and appreciate whatever there is, and join in praise to God, some of which praise we may suppose would be 'unvoiced' were it not for human beings. There are many creatures whose lives we cannot emulate – whales and albatrosses in and on and above the great oceans, for instance – but human beings have capacities special to them as social beings, most centrally the capacities of language and the complexities of music-making and making and re-making the ways in which we shape and re-shape our world of meanings. Saying and singing 'God' in more or less ceremonious ways are among our special contributions to the praise of God. In one of our oldest expressions of faith, The Apostles' Creed, we find the phrase 'communio sanctorum', helpfully ambiguous in its reference to 'sacred things' as to 'sacred persons' (though commonly translated as 'communion of saints'). Given what we have learned afresh and in different ways of our kinship with non-human

40 A version is included in 2005, *Common Worship: Daily Prayer*, London: Church House Publishing, p. 641.

sentient creatures, we broaden and deepen our understanding of the phrase in that our praise of God is on their behalf as it were as well as on our own.

Divine largesse: and mercy for our frailties

To be more precise, however, in the Christian tradition we say and sing 'Glory be to the Father, and to the Son, and to the Holy Spirit'. We come to learn that in whatever we get up to by way of verbal or non-verbal, imaginative or routine pattern-making, putting things in some sort of order, however provisional, fixing and re-arranging our concerns, finding and re-finding meaning, we are responding to God who makes godself known, seeking creatures, as in Genesis 3.9 in which God is portrayed as calling for God's human creatures in the garden of Eden. God both seeks creatures and makes it possible for them to respond to that search, and what we mean by 'spirituality' is how human beings become their best 'selves' in their response. God is present to us, and human beings are open to that 'presence', without being overwhelmed by it. The bush in the desert burned but was not consumed. For Exodus 3.14 is about the revelation of God as mercy. Given that human beings are capable of depths of malice not to be found elsewhere among God's creatures – malice inflicted not only on one another but on other creatures – it is a mercy that we are not finally left to flounder in our delusions and harms, some of them self-made, or in our downright wickedness. Frailty and weakness are at one end of the scale of what may precipitate us into trouble; muddle, lack of thought in advance, incompetence and laziness lurk somewhere along the line; indifference to the well-being of others in their hunger and deprivation, which we could remedy if we made it our priority; sheer deliberate infliction of pain just for the hell of it – from these we may be delivered by God's largesse of mercy, grace and transformative presence as 'Spirit'. This is 'sacramented', promised, pledged, sealed to us, and we are positively invited to 'party', to join in worship in the conviviality and companionship of a re-possessed paradise, encompassing more than we can imagine, and including the most astonishing variety of odd-balls, strangers, and 'nobodies', those we think are recognizably 'saintly', those creatures whose lives are akin but even more mysterious to us than we are to ourselves, all found among the sanctified.

We also remind ourselves of how we can make a mess of sacramentality, our being open to the transformative presence of God, however the sense of that presence comes to us. In other words, we respond to the divine promise, but to do this we need a graced confidence, certainly, but we also need to be wary of our own superstitions, our ability to grasp greedily at what we may think serves our interests, in what matters most to us and, above all, in our religion. It can be hard going to learn not to attribute to either things or other persons power or powers that they cannot have, and we need to be especially wary of our own self-pretensions. We do what we can to be and become alert to the mediation of divine presence transfiguring aspects of who and what we are, but we cannot precipitate it, cannot ourselves make God present.

The distinctively Christian conviction here has to do with the revelation to us of divine presence in the creativity of redemption, mercy and forgiveness, God's not merely flesh-and-blood making, but flesh-and-blood taking in the presence to us of Christ Jesus. In and through that presence God becomes 'sayable' through whatever we grasp of Christ's particular living, dying, and re-creation to life in God, in what we celebrate as 'Ascension'. God in mercy shows us God's knowing of what it is like to be human, not least what it is like to enjoy the full gamut of relationship from friendship and commitment to betrayal and abandonment. God is present but, as it were, concealed among us in the person of Christ. He, above all, is the sacrament of our hope in our communities both in this life and in the lives of the sanctified ones in the exuberance of paradise. And his Ascension signifies for us the renewed outpouring of the Spirit on God's creatures, the continuous availability of the resources we need in mercy for the transformation of our lives, the future kept open for the possibilities of better relationships, of a better world. Thus, Christian worship will include at some points the 'Kyrie eleison', the prayer for mercy, for in the worship of God revealed to us in Christ we align ourselves with the divine defeat of wickedness in ourselves and others, both in lamenting what we do, and in keeping sensitive to the presence of divine justice which we implement as best we can. Among the most difficult tasks for Christian worshippers are prayers of intercession for those who bring about evil, practising repentance for our own part in wrongdoing, and finding resources that help us be free of the worst and instead bolster our choice and our work for the best. So there is no room for self-satisfaction here. All depends on Christ, as two biblical texts suggest to us. As Psalm 68.18 has it: 'You have gone up on high and led captivity captive; you have received tribute, even from those who rebelled, that you might reign as Lord and God.' And at Hebrews 7.25 there is the promise that Christ 'ever lives to make intercession for us'.

Sacramental spirituality: specific practices

It takes time, much repetition, and specific and identifiable practices for this to become part of our lives. Communities keep together by sharing certain customs in the ordinary way of things, by people sharing insights with one another, by celebrating one another's achievements, holding festivals, learning to sing a national anthem, for instance, clearing the decks on particular days annually to meet and share life with one another. So those who worship God pay special attention to ensuring both that worship gets the space and time necessary, and that devotion to God receives public expression in their lives as a whole. That public expression is referred to as 'liturgy', public service – a point with which we will conclude in due course. It is because worship may be and often is deeply controversial, because it is concerned with matters of supreme importance in human life, that it may seem easier to try to avoid controversy by stifling it into a supposedly 'private' realm of life. Rather, we need to struggle to get it as right as we can and realize its integral connections with everything we have been, now are and may become. And, in the case of the Christian tradition, the narratives of God's flesh-taking in a particular person have over the course of time in different cultures, given a distinctive shape to Christian worship. Memorable Creeds give a frame of reference, and together with focus on the narratives of God's presence in a personal way in the incarnation, a whole pattern (which may be more or less elaborate) has been developed that frees us from thrashing about from scratch as it were. There always remains room for experiment as communities change in their times and places.

Our inherited traditions, however, make possible a certain selectivity and discrimination in attending to how we may become open to the divine presence in our living. We, so to speak, keep track of the divine creativity and generosity in mercy and redemption by specific sacraments, necessary if our 'sense of the sacramental' is not to disintegrate into incoherence. Whatever we do, our particular sacraments and our sense of the sacramental – in the most all-embracing sense – depend upon Christ in his glorified and ascended humanity continuing to be known as sacrament beyond our particular sacraments or our sensitivity to divine presence in a multitude of ways – sacramentality, embraced by the prayers of believing communities.

Specifically Christian communities are formed of those who respond to God as disciples, as indicated in John 15.12–17. The words 'Abide in me as I in you' are key here, to some extent familiar to us because of the ways in which we become fully human persons in intra-dependence with others – which is where we began our reflections. In discipleship, that inter-relationship is given a depth that may transform us, for here presented is Christ and his life-giving mission to others. In the fourth gospel, 'John' portrays Christ as having experienced a hard-won struggle to convey to others his sense of the presence of God, as, for instance in his conversation with the Samaritan woman in John 4, or the extraordinary progress he makes towards the tomb of Lazarus in John 11 or the foot-washing scene of John 13. More, and worse, is to come in his approach to death and his endurance of the full horror of torture and death. In John 15 and in many other gospel texts it becomes clear that some human beings are summoned to be particularly close to him, and he requests that they show to others the love that he has shown them.

Discipleship in most Christian communities is marked by a ceremony of transition – baptism, anointing and commitment – shifting us into a realm where renewed identity in community and new stability through change may be secured. Our focus here, however, is on 'table', for in most Christian communities participation in a table-ceremony is deemed to be integral to how disciples are sustained in their relation to God as revealed in Christ. At its heart is 'thanksgiving' – acknowledging the gracious presence on which all depends in creativity and mercy. Like baptism, at a certain level it is a ceremony and celebration of the ordinary, in that both baptism and eucharist have at their roots the washing and feeding, primary modes of caring for one another, without which no one can thrive, least of all the most vulnerable new-born establishing her or his presence among us. The phrase '*koinonia hagion*', commonly translated as 'Holy Communion', in its broadest sense has to do with making the common holy and the holy common. Human persons in and through their ordinary lives and activities may become open to divine presence, and that divine presence will be mediated to us through ordinary persons and ordinary things and activities, in which hospitality has a very special place, as we saw at the beginning of our reflections.

Christ providing and presiding

So far as the gospels are concerned, we find that the provision of hospitality to Christ and his disciples by all sorts and conditions of persons, sometimes at a festive occasion, could also be more or less fraught with significance as indeed mealtimes may be, depending on what is on offer, who sits where, what is said and remembered, what happens afterwards. Among the most extraordinary narratives in the gospels are the occasions after death and burial when Christ appears to share meals once more and indeed to act again as host as well as guest. Recollection of the last occasion on which he was host of a meal with a close group of disciples is coupled with the joy of recollected meals in and with his transformed presence (for example Acts 2.41–47). We can therefore grasp why the Christian eucharist – 'thanksgiving' – emerged in the earliest years in which Christians became a distinctive community, but it is by no means entirely clear to us just how it happened, even when we attend to early texts beyond Christian scriptures. We recall that these were put together over a considerable period of time in all sorts of different places, only gradually being accepted as authoritative as the Christian tradition became distinctive and there developed enough organization and agreement to decide what was authoritative and what had to be left on one side.

We can learn from Christian scriptures that new communities were formed in which major differences of status were gradually overcome and in which Christ was revered and experienced as divine, as the one who provides and presides over a celebration that disciples shared with one another and with him. This inevitably meant that disciples had to drop out of other celebrations that depended on other loyalties and commitments. Eating together and knowing what that meant distinguished Christian communities from other devout believers, but it seems to have taken a variety of forms, as one might expect, given the diversity of circumstances in which groups of Christians identified themselves and came together. Whatever form those meals took, however, and however formalized or not in ceremony, they were certainly to be distinguished from the meals and ceremonies of others. Two points remain clear enough. The eucharistic meal had its origin in an occasion of the utter betrayal of Christ's personal hospitality and of blundering, misplaced expressions of unsustainable loyalty by those who still had not learned that their lives depended on God's fidelity to them rather than on the inadequacies of their commitment to God (Psalm 41.9;

Luke 22.34 and parallels). The second point follows, that Christ's death was of a once-for-all character in putting human beings into a renewed relationship with God. And third, this conviction arose not simply from reflection on meals with him but on the connection of his words and actions at those meals and throughout his life in joy and dedication to God with his experience of betrayal, utter humiliation and a ghastly end. Many others suffered under the imperial power of his era, but in this particular life and death, in Christ's resurrection-and-ascension, human beings were and are invited to see a supreme manifestation of divine mercy, and of divine transformation of the worst that human beings can do to one another. So in the eucharist-meal disciples are held close to the course of their forgiveness and sanctification. One expression of the faith that developed over the centuries (found in a twelfth-century monastic text) reads in translation: 'O sacred banquet, in which Christ is received, the memory of his passion is renewed, the soul is filled with grace, and the pledge of future glory is given us.' These words do something to capture and express the experience of Christ ascended and present, the abundance and transformative presence of God's gracious Spirit, and God's merciful re-orientation of human persons towards flourishing and fulfilment.

Once more: ignore nothing!

If we delve into Christian tradition across the first millennium, however, we find that disciples were by no means necessarily limited to thinking only of the eucharistic meal when reflecting on how God might be present to them – that presence both revealed and mysteriously concealed. Particularly important is to notice the range of meaning of 'sacrament', which could cover saying the Prayer That Jesus Taught (cf. Matthew 6.9–13), saying a creed, making the sign of the cross, an actual baptismal font of whatever shape, the water used, the ashes of penitence, the oil of anointing, the gestures of blessing, a ceremony of foot-washing, as well as the reading and exposition of scripture and the practice of prayer. All this needs exploration and re-evaluation in our own situation, given what else we might list (virtually inexhaustible) as well as new liturgies we may devise, of which Harvest Festivals and Carol Services are just two examples. Great paintings, even when torn from their original context in churches, and hanging in galleries, may become the focus of prayer, as may many different forms of music, including settings of liturgy sung in concert halls and a significant range of other musical forms from Andrew Lloyd Webber's 'Jesus Christ Superstar' to John Coltrane's jazz composition 'A love supreme'. We have perhaps also recovered a sense of the importance of spaces, of gardens and the way in which they are set out, of how they relate to particular buildings and their disposition. There is much to explore and to reconsider. And while there is no one understanding of how divine word and human word are related in preaching, at the very least we acknowledge its importance in initiating and sustaining and developing sensitivity and response to God's generosity. We might also want to emphasize the need of the preacher to foster the 'discontinuity' of forgiveness, that is, of the possibilities of opening up the future so that we are neither finally defined by the wrongs we do nor the wrongs done to us. Not the least of our problems, however, is that our search for and expression of the 'sacramental', the mediation of the presence of God to us, can in certain circumstances become problematic, disturb us and irritate us as clutter that simply must be swept away so that we can see clearly again. Movements for 'reform' and resistance are sometimes of this kind, and we need to take them seriously. To the final phase of our reflections we now turn, with that point in mind.

Sacramentally sustained life

By the end of the first millennium, both constructive and problematic moves had been made in comprehending sacrament and sacramentality. In the western church in particular there developed a way of patterning one's life in relation to Christ in seven specific sacraments, related to birth, growth and strength, nutrition, sorting out inter-personal disorder, establishing reliable patterns of relationship and leaving one's present life. So baptism, confirmation, eucharist and penance, order and presidency, marriage and anointing for the transition from the death of this life into the life of resurrection would see human creatures through, as it were. The sacraments and the special virtues associated with them – faith, courage, charity, justice, prudence, temperance and hope – were the marks of a sacramentally sustained life, but the pattern was no sooner more or less established than it was fragmented when trust in divine promise was eroded, particularly evident in deep anxiety about the reality of God-given salvation and controversy about the eucharist. It is from the period of the Reformation and beyond that the western churches especially inherit major problems (which continue to arise) for relationships both with the Orthodox families of churches, and between the newer churches, and these problems continue to centre on what should be a ceremony of charity to one another which depends upon the presence of Christ.

Different ways of understanding what is going on in a ceremony of sacrament had been developed in the first millennium, and became sources of controversy and disagreement of the most bitter kind in the second, inevitably in connection with the eucharist-meal. One option was to maintain that human beings were united by faith in a saving relation with Christ ascended and glorified. Another option, however, was that because what was used in the ceremony (grain and grape transformed by the work of human hands) were consecrated by words, including the invocation of the triune God, the 'elements' used both remained what they appeared to be and also became a different reality. This latter conviction gave rise to new forms of worship, and to what to many seemed to be an unacceptable attribution of authority to the ordained, especially when that authority was also manifested in connection with contrition and forgiveness. That a sacrament is 'an outward and visible sign of an inward and spiritual grace given unto us', which is a 'means of grace', is a maxim that remains important, whichever option is defended – and both may properly be. Out of the period rich in controversy about so many matters, some Christians (for example, the Society of Friends, also known as Quakers) continue to embody one important principle. This is that the presence of Christ requires no mediation through ceremony or other persons, and is manifested in the transformed lives of disciples in private devotion, gathered meetings for worship in which silence is a most important practice, and the practice of the open table at a full meal not only with other disciples but with any in need of food or companionship. Among other matters of importance, the embodiment of this principle connects us to other forms of disciplined maturity, which may be represented in other ways by different expressions of discipleship, for example, the capacity to refuse what may consume and enslave us, so that we are freed up for the kinds of life that matter. It is also worth attending to the importance of leaving space and time for both hearing the stories and listening to the insights of those gathered for worship, of the many incidents of great importance, which have no pre-determined ceremony, that enable human beings to negotiate their lives, which will inevitably include experiences of grief and loss as well as of promise and delight.

Public service

Although not everyone will opt for the particular practices of the presence of Christ which eschew all ceremony except that of the most austere gathering together, what remains is the essential focus on Christ as the sacrament of salvation in gathering for the eucharist-meal, whatever form in detail this takes, the invocation of God's Spirit in sustaining relationship with one another, and maintaining openness for the future. Whatever the pattern or ceremony, we need constantly to insist that communities of disciples do not exist in and for themselves in an inward-turned way. Liturgy, as we recall, is 'public service' and at the conclusion of a liturgy we are instructed to 'go' – out to the world shared with and constituted by others, to the world of work and unemployment, of social participation or its deprivation, to the world in which remain starvation, deep-seated poverty, the disturbances precipitated by conflict, the trafficking of persons, including the very young, for work and for sexual exploitation, racism and the provocation of hatred. Communities of disciples thrive – or not – in local and international contexts, in the realms of the commercial as well as of the charitable – and those who gather at 'table' both exit from it to tackle what they can and must in their various spheres, and return to it to receive the gracious presence of Christ in their shared life together.

Sending

MARK IRELAND

Sending: missional spirituality

Some years ago when vicar of a parish on the edge of Accrington, Lancashire, I had the privilege of preaching and commissioning a member of our congregation who was answering a call from God to leave her family and all that was precious to her, to travel to Africa and serve as a nurse in a remote hospital in south-west Uganda. As we gathered round Ann and prayed over her with the laying on of hands, it was a profound experience of 'sending' one of our own number to share in front-line mission on behalf of all of us. When I later had the opportunity to visit Ann at Kisiizi hospital in Uganda, I discovered that her mission context was very different from what many of us back home had imagined. Unlike Accrington, 80 per cent of the population of Uganda identify themselves as born-again Christians, and often do so within moments of meeting you – 'Hello, my name is Grace and I have accepted Jesus as my personal saviour.'

As I write, Ann is still at Kisiizi, and has developed a wonderful ministry looking after the children's ward and training other nurses. However, my experience of Ann's sending and commissioning service challenges me to think about how we send and commission *every* member of our church congregation for mission – at least both evangelism and social action – in their own town and in their places of work. Few of those who work in Accrington or Telford (where I now serve) will have the privilege of being in a majority Christian environment from Monday to Friday. The 'mission field' is not somewhere geographically distant to which a few are called to go. It is on our doorstep. All God's people (of all ages) are called to share with God in the costly divine mission to, and in, the world.

I remember years ago hearing someone say on the radio that if we really took Jesus' words seriously we would come to receive the eucharist on a Sunday drained and exhausted, holding out shaking hands like an alcoholic person gasping for a drink. We cannot with integrity share broken bread and wine outpoured and then return to our comfortable homes as if we have somehow done our religious duty. The eucharist is our refuelling point on the missionary journey, and the sending part of the communion service is akin to the moment when we leave the motorway services (note the word) and need to be pointed in the right direction and helped to rejoin the fast-moving traffic.

Sending away the seekers?

We must be careful, however, in how we do the 'Sending' at the end of the eucharist, lest we give the impression that the locus of mission is only to be found beyond the door of the church. The evidence is that a significant proportion of people who attend worship on a typical Sunday are themselves seekers rather than committed disciples. A research project in the deanery of Almondsbury in Wakefield diocese showed that while the average Sunday attendance for the 17 churches totalled 620, over a typical eight-week period (avoiding major festivals) the total number of individuals who attended worship was actually 3,432. Only 144 attended on all eight Sundays, and a staggering 1,176 attended only once. If this deanery is in any way typical, this suggests that the vast majority of the people who attend Anglican churches over any two-month period are people who do so occasionally or infrequently.

The evidence also shows that for most seekers, belonging comes before believing, as John Finney demonstrated in his ground-breaking book *Finding Faith Today*.[41] For the majority of people, becoming a Christian is a process rather than an event, and happens after the individual has begun to attend a place of worship rather than before. At the eucharist we need to enable conversations between those who are regulars and those who are enquirers or searchers. Research also shows that once a person begins to attend church, if they begin to form

41 This point is the major theme of John Finney, 1992, *Finding Faith Today: How Does it Happen?*, Swindon: Bible Society.

relationships with six other church members over the next six weeks they are likely to continue to come; otherwise they are likely to leave and not return. This has major implications for how we dismiss a congregation at the end of a service. We need to do so in a way that helps build supportive relationships among those within the church building, who may be at very different stages of faith, as well as commissioning people to engage with those outside – who may not be nearly as receptive as those who have tentatively taken the first step of coming along to a church service.

Recent writing on the origins of the eucharist have stressed the fact that much of Jesus' ministry was conducted over meals, so much so that he was accused of being a 'glutton and a drunkard, a friend of tax collectors and sinners' (Luke 7.34). Unlike the Pharisees, Jesus had few if any rules about the company he kept at meal times. As Stephen Burns writes, 'Hospitality seems to be the key point of meals for Jesus; his own meals were marked by inclusion rather than exclusion.'[42] How do we square this with our own carefully fenced eucharistic tables, where a welcome is often extended only to 'those who are already communicant members of their own churches' (as the invitation to communion is commonly heard in English parish churches), and where someone searching for faith is likely to feel exclusion rather than inclusion? Even when the presider tries hard to include

---

42 Stephen Burns, 2006, *Living the Thanksgiving: Exploring the Eucharist* (Church Times Study Guides), Norwich: Canterbury Press, p. 2.

the non-communicant, perhaps inviting them to bring a service book or service sheet to the rail as a sign that they are welcome to receive a blessing, it can seem only to reinforce the message of exclusion.

The importance of this question is heightened by the success of the Liturgical Movement in restoring the eucharist to its central place as the main act of worship on a Sunday morning. Before the rise of the Liturgical Movement the main morning service was Mattins, a morning service of the word, with the eucharist being available (apart from festivals) mostly at 8 a.m. or as an 'add-on' for those who wished to stay behind after Mattins. In this situation, the main morning service was at least open to all – even if, some of us might imagine, rather dreary! The trend of increased frequency of communion at the main morning service has come exactly at the same time as the proportion of the population who are confirmed has plummeted. Such a situation cries out for a much more open table, and a willingness to let people (at least baptized people) receive the eucharist as an immediate response to the Word proclaimed – food for their spiritual journey to, as well as in, the faith.

Sending and fresh expressions of church

Damian Feeney, called to be a mission priest in a new housing estate in Preston, began by celebrating the eucharist in the foyer of the Asda supermarket at 9.30 a.m. on a Sunday morning, as people tended to gather there waiting for the store to open. Remembering Wesley's description of communion as 'a converting ordinance', this missionary practice highlights the fact that the eucharist is more than food for the faithful – perhaps even an invitation to 'taste and see that the Lord is gracious' (Psalm 34.8). Driving some large distances to preach in my previous role as a missioner, I noticed that the other places that draw significant gatherings on a Sunday morning are car boot sales and cemeteries. When churches plan mission weekends (as many still do), perhaps we should dare to think of taking our worship out to places such as these.

Could an occasional part of the 'Sending' be to take the celebration of the eucharist out of the church building on Sunday morning to where other people are gathering? The missiologist George Lings identifies one of the significant steps in reaching non-churched people today as 'The going of come and the coming of go', challenging the church to move from a 'come to us' model of mission to 'let us go to you'.

Mission-shaped eucharist

In his book *Liquid Church*,[43] Pete Ward writes about the need for church to adopt whatever shape is suited to fit the surrounding culture, while retaining its essential

43 Pete Ward, 2002, *Liquid Church*, Carlisle: Paternoster Press, has been an influential vision for moving beyond what he calls 'one-size-fits-all' worship. For some discussion of Ward on worship, see Stephen Burns, 'Mission-shaped Worship', *Anvil* 21 (2005), pp. 185–201.

nature.[44] This is some of the thinking that has helped to shape fresh expressions of church. In a liquid church a neat and clear 'dismissal' may be out of place. Perhaps what we can all learn from fresh expressions of church is that we may need more fuzzy beginnings and endings to our services, so that worship arises out of its context, and so that worship fuses into mission.

Fashion or foundation?

Is the decision to devote a whole chapter in a book on the eucharist to the Sending simply a contemporary Anglican fad, seeking to make everything 'mission-shaped', or does it express something at the very heart of what the eucharist is?

At the Last Supper Jesus clearly looks back to the exodus, made present in the Passover meal, and also forward, to the final consummation of all things: 'I have eagerly desired to eat this Passover with you before I suffer, for I tell you, I will not eat it until it is fulfilled in the dominion of God' (Luke 22.15–16). The missional nature of the eucharist is rooted in its eschatological dimension, holding present and future together. This theme is picked up in the *Methodist Worship Book*'s post-communion prayer, which is also included in *Common Worship*:

---

44 See also Stephen Burns, 2008, 'Heaven or Las Vegas? Engaging Liturgical Theology' in Pete Ward, ed., *Mass Culture: The Interface of Eucharist and Mission*, Oxford: Bible Reading Fellowship, pp. 95–112.

We thank you, Lord,
that you have fed us in this sacrament,
united us with Christ,
and given us a foretaste of the heavenly banquet
prepared for all people.[45]

To receive holy communion points us forward to the consummation of God's purposes, and therefore commissions us to be agents of transformation in the world. The eucharist is, as J. A. T. Robinson put it, *the* distinctive Christian social action – all else flows from it.[46] Or, as Bishop Frank Weston once put it in his stirring address to the Anglo-Catholic Congress of 1923:

> If you are prepared to fight for the right of adoring Jesus in his Blessed Sacrament, then you have got to come out from before your Tabernacle and walk, with Christ mystically present in you, out into the streets of this country and find the same Jesus in the people of your cities and villages. You cannot worship Jesus in the Tabernacle if you do not pity Jesus in the slum ... Go out and look for Jesus in the ragged, in the naked, and in the oppressed and sweated, in those who have lost hope, in those who are struggling to make good. Look for Jesus. And when you see him, gird yourself with his towel and try to wash his feet.[47]

---

45 E.g. *Methodist Worship Book*, p. 197. The prayer is also included as a supplementary text in *Common Worship*, p. 297.

46 A major theme throughout J. A. T. Robinson, 1960, *Liturgy Coming to Life*, London: Mowbray.

47 Quoted in David Stancliffe, 2003, *A Pilgrim Prayerbook*, London: Continuum, p. 108.

The eschatological nature of the eucharist also calls us to proclamation and evangelism. In the earliest account of the institution of the eucharist we read, 'For as often as you eat this bread and drink the cup, you proclaim the Lord's death until he comes' (1 Corinthians 11.26). We cannot share in the bread and wine of Christ's messianic banquet and remain indifferent to the millions around us living and dying without the knowledge of God's saving love in Christ. We cannot eat the bread without realizing that we *are* what we are invited to receive, the body of Christ, broken for the sake of the world. As Jesus prayed for his disciples in the upper room, 'As you sent me into the world, I have sent them into the world' (John 17.18), so we are called to share his message. Indeed, Jesus has already prayed for those who will believe because of those like us: 'I ask not only on behalf of these, but also on behalf of those who will believe in me through their word . . .' (John 17.20).

The gospel of John speaks not only of the 'sending' of the Son, but also of the Son's 'return' to the Father. As a recent report of the Liturgical Commission reminds us, the movement of God's mission is both a sending and a returning, a reaching-out and a gathering-in in order to restore all things in Christ (Colossians 1.15–20).[48] This double movement is reflected in our worship. When we gather to worship we 'return' to God in praise and penitence, and in communion, and are sent out by God

---

48 Liturgical Commission, 2007, *Transforming Worship: Living the New Creation* (GS 1651) London: Church House Publishing.

to engage with God's transforming work in the world. However the 'going out' at the end of the liturgy itself looks forward to a final 'return' when Christ will come again in power and glory to perfect a new creation.

This double movement of returning and sending is found in the Old Testament too. It was in the context of worship that Isaiah of Jerusalem heard his call to mission: '"Whom shall I send, and who will go for us?" And I said, "Here am I; send me!"' (Isaiah 6.8). Worship is not a means of escape from the world; rather, it enables us to see God as God is, and to see the world as God sees it. And once we glimpse the world as God sees it, we are impelled to share in the divine mission of transformation. Truly Spirit-filled worship both touches heaven and changes earth!

Baptism and eucharist

At the licensing of a mission priest who was being called to form church among unchurched young adults in Stoke-on-Trent, the bishop commented that the sacramental focus of the priest's ministry would, at least initially, be baptismal rather than eucharistic. Although I can see the point the bishop was making, there is a danger in seeing one sacrament as primarily nourishing the faithful and the other as missionary. The two sacraments are interdependent, and dividing them risks distorting their meaning.[49] In the eucharist, as members of the

49 See J. G. Davies, 1966, *Worship and Mission*, London: SCM Press, pp. 92–112.

church, we offer ourselves, 'our souls and bodies',[50] in union with the unique sacrifice of Christ, and so renew the consecration to mission that was made at our baptism. As we feed on Christ in the eucharist we are helped to become what we already are through the gift of our baptism: the adopted children of God. This raises important questions about how we celebrate the eucharist in fresh expressions of church.

The Latin word *sacramentum* was the word used of the 'pledge' or 'oath' that a Roman soldier took to his general to serve him in battle no matter what the cost. Thus, to receive the *sacraments* (both baptism and eucharist) means to commit oneself to strive in the service of Christ – as is made explicit in the Baptism service, where candidates are committed

> to fight valiantly as a disciple of Christ
> against sin, the world and the devil,
> and remain faithful to Christ to the end of your life.[51]

Mass and mission

The words 'mass' and 'mission' are clearly linked. The dismissal rite in Latin was called the *missa*, from the

---

50 See the post-communion prayer in *Common Worship*, p. 182.

51 2005, *Common Worship: Christian Initiation*, London: Church House Publishing, p. 68. Note that the version of these words found in the earlier *Alternative Service Book 1980* (*ASB*) was even stronger: 'to fight valiantly under the banner of Christ against sin, the world, and the devil, and continue his faithful soldiers and servants to the end of your lives'.

words with which it ended, *Ite, missa est*, and this eventually gave its name to the whole rite. It is significant that in the Roman Catholic tradition the sacrament of the new covenant takes its name from the dispersal at the end.

The link between 'mass' and mission deserves lively thought – which is what Stephen Cottrell offers in a memorable metaphor, as follows: 'The eucharist is not the hot bath at the end of the day, when we lie back and forget all our troubles, it is more like the cold shower at the beginning of the day to zap us and energise us for what lies ahead.'[52] For as David Bosch wrote:

> Mission has its origin in the heart of God. God is a fountain of sending love. This is the deepest source of mission. It is impossible to penetrate deeper still: there is mission because God loves people.[53]

The *Mission-shaped Church* report affirms these perspectives: 'It's not the church of God that has a mission in the world, but the God of mission who has a church in the world.'[54]

---

52 Stephen Cottrell, 2001, 'The Dismissal' in Stephen Conway, ed., *Living the Eucharist: Affirming Catholicism and the Liturgy*, London: Darton, Longman & Todd, pp. 122–6, p. 125. For Stephen Cottrell's lively ideas on eucharist as 'encounter' see 2006, *From the Abundance of the Heart: Catholic Evangelism for All Christians*, London: Darton, Longman & Todd, pp. 110–14 (and 98–9).

53 David Bosch, 1991, *Transforming Mission*, Maryknoll, NY: Orbis, p. 392.

54 Tim Dearborn, quoted in 2004, *Mission-shaped Church*, London: Church House Publishing, p. 103.

Feeding before sending

In Mark's account of the call of the twelve disciples, their first calling is to be with Jesus, listed before the call to go out and preach and heal (Mark 3.14). Jesus taught and fed the five thousand before he sent them away. Jesus healed the sick before he sent them away. Jesus told his disciples to wait for the gift of the Spirit before sending them out to proclaim God's reign.

In the words of institution at the Last Supper in both the gospels of Mark and Matthew Jesus says first to his chosen disciples, 'Take and eat; this is my body' before he says, 'This is my blood of the covenant which is poured out for many.'[55] The slight difference between the words about the bread and the cup may be significant, as Timothy Radcliffe has suggested. The bread is given just to the disciples. The cup is also given to them, but is poured out for the many. There is here a tension, as in every eucharist, between the gathering into communion of the disciples, those close to Jesus, and the reaching out to all for the fullness of God's reign. 'The challenge is to keep alive the dynamic tension between the cup and the bread, between the gathering into community and the outreach to all humanity . . . This is the breathing of the Church, the gathering in of breath and its expulsion.'[56] There is a sense in which we need to receive for ourselves before we are ready to invite others to receive from the table. Church members need to

55 Matthew 26.26, 28. Note in original.

56 Timothy Radcliffe, OP, 2006, *What is the Point of Being a Christian?* London: Continuum, p. 178.

experience what it is to be loved and known intimately before they can go out to others.

The church is called to be a worshipping missionary community – for the mission to happen there has to be a real sense of worship and community, as Robert Warren explained in his ground-breaking book *Building Missionary Congregations.*[57] I owe a huge amount to Robert's insights and inspiration; however, I have always been just a little uncomfortable with the title of that particular book, believing that what we are called first of all to create are not 'missionary congregations' but 'worshipping communities'. It is, I believe, the encounter with a truly worshipping community that both attracts the outsider in and also impels the insider to go out with the good news.

'Sending' in *Common Worship*

Is the post-communion part of the eucharist the anticlimax of the rite – the closing prayer and dismissal – or is it the com*mission*ing for ministry and service?

Compared with the length of the eucharistic prayer, the commissioning for ministry and service at the end of the rite is very brief, just nine words – 'Go in peace to love and serve the Lord' – and these words can be abbreviated still further to remove all reference to service.

57 See Robert Warren, 1995, *Building Missionary Congregations*, London: Church House Publishing, pp. 20–3, where Robert depicts three interlocking circles: worship, community and mission.

Interestingly, the *Common Worship* baptism service uses the notion of a 'commission' straight after the sacramental action, to underline the responsibilities of congregation, parents and godparents. I wonder, could we not make more of this and make the commissioning of the congregation a more visible part of the post-communion liturgy at the eucharist? The questions suggesting the shape of Christian life from the commissioning in the baptism service itself seem to be an obvious resource to explore:

Will you continue in the apostles' teaching and fellowship,
in the breaking of bread, and in the prayers?
With the help of God, I will.

Will you persevere in resisting evil,
and, whenever you fall into sin, repent and return to the Lord?
With the help of God, I will.

Will you proclaim by word and example
the good news of God in Christ?
With the help of God, I will.

Will you seek and serve Christ in all people,
loving your neighbour as yourself?
With the help of God, I will.

Will you acknowledge Christ's authority over human society,

by prayer for the world and its leaders,
by defending the weak, and by seeking peace and justice?
With the help of God, I will.[58]

If, as Richard Giles suggests,[59] much of the gathering may be oriented around the font, use of texts like the baptismal commissioning might encourage us back to the font for the sending, so that we think of expressions of sharing in God's mission as our baptismal way of life.

As it stands, the post-communion rite in *Common Worship* is much abbreviated from the Book of Common Prayer's provisions, which included the Lord's Prayer, a choice of two very long after-communion prayers, the Gloria and the blessing. Although much shorter, the two alternative *Alternative Service Book 1980* prayers after communion had a much stronger 'mission' emphasis than the prayer book, written as it was very much in a Christendom context. The first *ASB* prayer, with its memorable echoes of the parable of the prodigal son/forgiving father in Luke 15.11–32, is rich with further biblical allusion, asking:

May we who share Christ's body live his risen life;
we who drink his cup bring life to others;
we whom the Spirit lights give light to the world.

---

58 *Common Worship: Christian Initiation*, p. 73. See also, for example, *Common Worship*, pp. 55 and 152 and 2005, *Common Worship: Daily Prayer*, London: Church House Publishing, p. 313.

59 Richard Giles, 2004, *Creating Uncommon Worship: Transforming the Liturgy of the Eucharist*, Norwich: Canterbury Press, pp. 102–4.

The second prayer contained the stirring petition, 'Send us out in the power of the Spirit to live and work to your praise and glory.' These two prayers, with their vivid and memorable imagery, have clearly struck a chord with congregations, and have been included unamended in *Common Worship*. However, with the advent of a whole raft of new post-communion prayers, the use of one of them is sadly, in my view, no longer mandatory.

The distinctive contribution of the Presbyterian and Reformed churches to the emerging ecumenical consensus on the fourfold shape of the eucharist has been to give increased emphasis and space to the Sending. Some churches' liturgies now include an explicit 'word of mission' as the first part of the order under the fourth major heading – for example, the Uniting Church in Australia includes Matthew 28.19–20 and suggests other possible passages 'or words from the psalm or other reading for the day'.[60] The invited pause[61] for silent devotion before the post-communion prayer is a time when I have instinctively often repeated a Bible verse from the gospel or from the sermon for meditation before leading into the prayer – and so I find it exciting to discover that many churches now do the same in some form or another. In the Church of England, *Common Worship* had abandoned the *Alternative Service Book 1980* practice of including a sentence of scripture or 'word of mission' before the post-communion prayer – where a verse

60 2005, *Uniting in Worship* 2, Sydney: Uniting Church Press, p. 223.

61 Note the sometimes overlooked rubric, '*Silence is kept*', in *Common Worship*, p. 182.

of scripture was expected at that point, although it was not called a 'word of mission'. However, in *Common Worship: Times and Seasons* 'dismissal gospels' are now provided for each liturgical season, encouraging congregations to recover this valuable opportunity to hear a final few verses of scripture before being sent out into the world.[62]

The practice of sending

In my experience, the fairly sparse liturgical provision for the Sending in *Common Worship* is often further abbreviated because of pressure of time – perhaps in a large busy church because the service has overrun, or perhaps in a small church because the priest has to hurry on to preside at another church within his or her care.

To my mind, too often an over-long distribution is compensated for by an over-brief 'sending'. And yet I know the pressures for myself: I have recently moved to be vicar of a fairly large evangelical church; in the parish profile due emphasis was given to the church's strong preaching tradition, and yet I was intrigued to discover that more time in the morning service was taken up with the distribution of the elements to the people than with the sermon. If enough people are involved in the distribution and the sidespersons are well briefed, then a large congregation should be able to receive communion in an unhurried way without overly prolonging the service at

62 2006, *Common Worship: Times and Seasons*, London: Church House Publishing, pp. 42, 87, etc.

the expense of the dismissal.[63] An over-long distribution time can be the time of 'the fidget factor', when people lose concentration and have disengaged before the critical moment of commissioning for service.

And, I wonder, has the sending part of the liturgy also suffered as a result of the increasing custom of serving coffee after the service? More and more, congregations are not so much bidden to 'go in peace to love and serve the Lord' but rather 'stay and have a cup of coffee with us in the hall'. While the reasons for this are laudable, it does send out mixed messages and blunt the missionary moment.

Some practical ideas for enhancing the sending

Word of mission/last gospel

At the end of the distribution, perhaps use a few verses from one of the scripture passages for the day, or another suitable and short Bible passage, as a focus for meditation before leading a prayer of commissioning for service. Obvious scriptures include: Micah 6.8; Matthew 5.14, 16; Acts 1.8; Romans 12.1; 1 Corinthians 16.13, 14; Colossians 3.17. And we need to be imaginative about finding many ways to engage the young: they might be invited to receive the word of mission as downloads to their iPods and emails, allowing a sense of being sent to echo through the week.

---

63 For lots of ideas about creative ways to share communion, see Richard Giles, *Creating Uncommon Worship*, pp. 199–201.

Post-communion prayer

For a congregation who use PowerPoint or some other form of overhead projection, how about bringing up on the screen images of church members going about their daily work, both paid and unpaid? Imagine saying the words 'send us out in the power of the Spirit to live and work to your praise and glory' with different pictures behind the words, of Gill the postwoman delivering the post, or Andrew the teacher in front of his class, or Ian the mechanic fixing a lorry, or Valerie at home caring for a dependent relative. Perhaps we could ask church members to send in photos of themselves in their place of work.

Tools of our trade

How about if at the preparation of the table people bring forward the tools of their trade – a checkout assistant's name badge, a doctor's stethoscope, a café server's order pad, and so on – so that they, alongside other gifts, are presented at the holy table for blessing? They could then be taken in procession at the end of the service so that our bodies' movement from gathering and sending is mirrored in this use of symbols of our daily life. This practice could be further strengthened by the congregation turning to face the deacon or presider as he or she gives the dismissal from the church door, so that the people intentionally make the gesture of turning to face 'the world' God loves.

Blessing

There is a tradition in the Orthodox Church that the congregation stands holding out their hands in front of them as the priest gives the final blessing, which – at least in churches where the congregation are not holding books – could be a visual way of receiving God's empowering and blessing for the work of mission. A moving variation on this Orthodox practice might be to invite members of the congregation to stand and turn to face the direction of their place of work (paid or unpaid, office or home) before the blessing is pronounced.

Moving the 'offertory'

In Justin Martyr's earliest account of Christian worship[64] offerings are collected for the poor, the sick, those in prison and the sojourner at the end of the service after the distribution of the bread and wine. Recovering this primitive position for the offertory on occasion might strengthen the link between receiving from God and being sent out to share in God's mission in the world. An interesting variation is the practice at St Mark's, Capitol Hill, Washington DC, where at the preparation of the table, along with the eucharistic elements, the people present at the table large baskets of ingredients required for that week's soup kitchen for the homeless on the streets of Washington (the recipe having been advertised on the previous Sunday's pew bulletin).

---

64 See Stephen Burns' introductory essay, above, on 'the journey through the liturgy', pp. 4–5.

Children and young people

I have sometimes heard adults complain about young people using mobile phones in church, but, I wonder, is there not space to try ways of using such technology creatively? If a strong visual image is used in a service – maybe a large painting or picture or display – why not encourage those with mobile phones to take a picture of it at the end of the service and use it as the 'wallpaper' on their phone during the week to remind them of the theme of the service? Or, how about encouraging everyone with mobile phones to text a nominated person to receive a group text with the word of mission on their phones as they leave church?

We need to be conscious also that for some children and young people the experience of 'Sending' comes much earlier in the service, as they are sent out of the worship area to children's groups. In many churches there is a tradition of trying to re-engage the children and young people at the end of the service, by asking them to show or tell what they have been doing in Sunday school. While laudable in intent, this can come over as slightly patronizing – rather like the prayer for the children before they go off to their groups earlier in the service. In my previous church we experimented with asking one of the children to pray for the adults staying in the service as well as having an adult pray for the children going out. Likewise, rather than just asking the children what they have learnt in their groups, how about asking one or two adults to tell the children – in two or three accessible sentences – what they have been learning during the sermon? It might be a revelation for the preacher, as well as affirming the principle that Christians are never too old to learn. I also know of at least one church where the decision was made for the children to stay in the main worship area for a period of weeks, while the adults went out to the hall each week for the sermon slot. As well as demonstrating that children are as much a part of the church as the grown-ups, it also made the grown-ups think again about the quality of the facilities they provided for the young!

Sharing peace

One strong way of affirming the fact that the Sending Out begins with those in church, is to make the greeting of peace the last word of worship. *Common Worship* clearly allows for this.[65] And of course in the Book of Common Prayer a word of peace is part of the blessing at the end of the service (echoing Philippians 4.7 – 'The peace of God which passeth all understanding . . .'). Having recovered the peace as an active part of the service rather than a passive receiving, perhaps the next step is, at least on occasion, to move the greeting to after the blessing, so that it becomes a real engagement between members of the congregation (not least as it is made up – hopefully – of both seekers and settlers in the church community, both 'core' and 'fringe' church members) rather than a stylized greeting that carries no opportunity for further conversation? Perhaps we might

---

65 *Common Worship*, p. 333, note 16.

imagine the presider offering an invitation something like this: 'Go and find someone you don't know, find out their name, offer them the peace, and take them for coffee . . .'

This is what happens in the church of which I am the minister. We are experimenting with giving the peace the last (formal) word of the service, so that rather than just a stylized 'Peace be with you' spoken to a stranger, members of the congregation are encouraged to seek out someone whose name they don't know, introduce themselves and invite that person to join them for a coffee. And we are discovering that visitors to church often find this more inclusive and less threatening than being approached in the middle of a service by people they don't know and with whom it is hard to initiate any kind of relationship in the brief moment before the offertory hymn is announced. It seems that sharing the peace after the blessing makes for a rather 'fuzzy' end to the service, but it does give space for pastoral and missional relationships to be formed (and it also has the bonus of reducing queues for coffee! – people drift gradually to the coffee table or to the door rather than all at once).

Dismissal

Where the peace is not given the last word, the emphatic final word of worship belongs to the dismissal. Most commonly in use in the Church of England is the commission to 'Go in peace to love and serve the Lord.' Alongside this, it is interesting to note various alternatives employed in other traditions. For example, the

Evangelical Lutheran Church in America has revived an old Huguenot sending out at this point: 'Go in peace. Remember the poor.'[66] And a fine example has also emerged in the new Baptist prayer book, *Gathering for Worship*. The leader announces, 'Our worship is ended,' to which the people respond 'Our service begins.'[67]

Prayer ministry after the service

In a growing number of churches, people are available at the end of the service to offer individual prayer on request, often with the laying on of hands. While the focus of this ministry is often on healing and wholeness, many people also seem to value the opportunity to bring all sorts of requests for prayer – for example, for wisdom about a difficult decision to be made at work, or for a job interview taking place that week. In such opportunities worship blends into the rest of the week, and the rest of life, in the kind of way I am suggesting the sending encourages.

These are just a few of many ideas and examples of good practice flowing from the sending that can help us to make the connections between our prayer and our daily life, between our worship and our work, and between our liturgies and our mission. Just as the rhythm of breathing in and out is essential for human life, so the gathering of God's people for worship and our sending

66 2006, *Evangelical Lutheran Worship*, Minneapolis, MN: Augsburg Fortress Press, pp. 115, 137.

67 2005, *Gathering for Worship: Patterns and Prayers for the Community of Disciples*, Norwich: Canterbury Press, p. 21.

out to be part of God's mission in the world are the essential rhythm of Christian discipleship. This is our true longing as Christians: for worship that touches heaven and changes earth.

Appendix 1

A note on using this book to support preaching

Christian people think their thoughts in constant interaction with scripture, which Anglican tradition – sustained by the practice of daily prayer – encourages us to engage daily. Each author in this volume makes reference to a number of scripture passages to shape and support their reflections. And it may be that readers who are preachers wish to engage the themes of this volume in their preaching ministry (not least at a time when the 'sacramental belonging' of children is being enlarged to include their full participation in the eucharist, and the challenges and opportunities of inviting children's participation sometimes requires robust catechesis for the young and their elders alike).

The following notes suggest options for drawing out the eucharistic themes of this volume in preaching at the eucharist.

Lectionary provisions and permissions

In the Church of England, 'following the lectionary' involves considerable freedoms, and these are often not appreciated. Although 'authorized lectionary provision [is] not a matter for local decision except where that provision permits',[68] that 'except' permits wide variation: *Common Worship* outlines the rule that during the Christmas cycle (from Advent Sunday through to Candlemas) and the Easter cycle (from Ash Wednesday through to Pentecost) and on Trinity Sunday and All Saints' Day, the prescribed readings must be used.[69] However, outside those times – all of 'ordinary time' and, therefore, a majority of each year – local lectionaries may be produced 'for pastoral reasons or preaching or teaching purposes'.[70] The creation of a local scripture reading scheme requires 'consultation' between the parish church council and minister, but is entirely permissible. Furthermore, *New Patterns for Worship* suggests some avenues of departure from the 'set' readings, and models the construction of local reading and sermon series. 'Section C' of *New Patterns for Worship*, the teaching resource for the *Common Worship* range, provides numerous forms of 'modular Bible readings'.[71] These tend to focus in on particular canonical books or portions of books, or take thematic approaches to particular subjects. *New Patterns for Worship* suggests that churches constructing local lectionaries 'should ensure that an adequate amount of Scripture is chosen; that justice is done to the balance of the book and to the general

---

68 *Common Worship*, p. 332.
69 *Common Worship*, p. 540.
70 *Common Worship*, p. 540.
71 2002, *New Patterns for Worship*, London: Church House Publishing, pp. 98–122.

teaching of Scripture; that appropriate Gospel passages are included if the services include Holy Communion; and that the PCC or an appropriate lay group is involved in the decisions'.[72] These are good guidelines to bear in mind in constructing local patterns of reading to help congregations explore the meanings of the eucharist, as anything else.

Suggesting specific passages that might be read to invite the assembly's reflection on the themes of gathering, word, table and sending seems to go 'against the grain' of *Common Worship* and *New Patterns for Worship*'s emphasis on local circumstances, pastoral or pedagogical. Hence, I resist such an uncontextualized approach here. But having said that, lections for 'Bible Sunday'[73] and Corpus Christi[74] are very obvious places to begin in relation to word and table. Otherwise, preachers might begin with the scriptures to which the authors in this volume especially refer in order to construct a sequence of readings for Christian assembly. Certainly, there is room to move in this direction within the freedoms and constraints offered by *Common Worship* and noted above.

72 *New Patterns for Worship*, p. 106.

73 *Common Worship*, p. 575.

74 *Common Worship*, p. 563.

Appendix 2

Questions for reflection and conversation

Common Worship indicates that 'the term "sermon" includes less formal exposition, the use of drama, interviews, discussion, audio-visuals and the insertion of hymns or other sections of the service between parts of the sermon' which may come before or after one of the readings or prayers.[75] In each case, the sermon (in the narrow sense) is only one means of engaging the word, and a whole ecology of ways of appropriating and responding to scripture is suggested. This kind of diversification of means of communication and appropriation is increasingly important in order to help people to hear and respond to the scriptures. Yet this in itself may not be enough. Home groups and study groups, and in some places, all-age Sunday school classes of some kind may be essential to support lifelong learning in the faith. The following are intended as *examples* of questions that might be used or adapted and discussed in home groups and all-age Sunday schools – or, in contexts where it is

75 See *Common Worship*, p. 27; cf. p. 332 (note 'on occasion').

appropriate, as beginnings to discussion that may complement or replace a monological sermon. The questions may also be used by individual readers to focus their engagement with particular chapters in this collection. They are certainly not the only questions that might be asked, and they may well not be 'right' for certain contexts; rather, they are intended as an encouragement to readers to 'mine' the material in this book for themselves.

Gathering

1. Richard turns Woody Allen's phrase that '95 per cent of life is showing up'. How important (or not) is being on time for worship? Why are you (or others) late? How are you (or they) welcomed, even so?
2. Richard suggests that 'gathering for eucharist provides us with the potential for communal action that can help transform society'. How does this happen?
3. Richard writes of the self-control and courage required to gather in robust community; yet 'on the simple act of gathering . . . depends the future of the church'. How do you relate to these assertions?
4. Consider Richard's design guidelines for gathering space. How might the buildings your community uses for worship be made more hospitable?

Word

1. Nicola sketches a broad canvas to introduce her theme of 'word'. How obvious or helpful is this for you?

2. Nicola discusses barriers and hindrances that frustrate us from hearing God's word, as well as habits that help clear space for listening. How are you helped in your struggles with the word?
3. Nicola suggests a range of ways of engaging the word in preaching and other activities. What do you think?
4. Nicola highlights the importance of commitment to diversity and inclusion if the word is to gain a wide hearing. How could this commitment be amplified in your community?

Table

1. Ann places emphasis on being 'at table' at church and also elsewhere. Have you thought about the extra/ordinariness of eating with others?
2. Ann suggests that we 'say grace' not only for whatever food might be on the table, but for our life as God's creatures. Do you practise this kind of thanksgiving? How might you start?
3. Ann mentions a number of specific liturgical practices that may be part of our celebration of eucharist – such as singing the *Sanctus* or the *Gloria*, saying psalms or canticles – and reminds us of the wide sense of the sacramental conveyed to us by Christian forebears – with the sign of the cross, fonts, oil and water, among other things, being important. What practices stir your own feeling of God's generosity?
4. Ann invites us to think into the gifts of creation (God's 'flesh-and-blood making') and incarnation (God's 'flesh-and-blood taking'). Would it be helpful

to keep this in mind during the eucharistic prayer's particular memory of Jesus' giving of his 'body/flesh' and 'blood'?

5. Ann reminds us of the importance of the meaning of 'liturgy' as 'public service'. How do you make connections between common worship and the common good?

Sending

1. Mark is concerned not to send away 'seekers'. How might your community enact this same concern?
2. Mark encourages the practice of an 'open' table, and yet speaks of the sacraments as acts of commitment. How would you negotiate this tension?
3. Mark suggests mission opportunities where churches might, on occasion, relocate opportunities for worship to places where others gather on Sunday mornings, such as supermarkets and cemeteries. Have you considered this?
4. Mark appeals for a more robust and creative 'Sending' section of the eucharistic service. What ideas of Mark, or your own, might your community do well to try?

Journey

1. How familiar to you is the *Common Worship* structure of gathering, word, table, sending?
2. If your community uses a locally produced order of service, does it distinguish the sections? Is it/would it be helpful?

3. How do the different sections of the eucharistic service relate to one another?
4. How might an appreciation of the journey through the liturgy enrich us spiritually?

About the Contributors

Richard Giles has recently retired to Tynemouth. He has served in parish ministry in the dioceses of Newcastle, Peterborough and Wakefield and was Canon Theologian of Wakefield Cathedral, before becoming Dean of Philadelphia, PA, USA (1999–2008). His publications include *How to Be an Anglican: Let Me Count the Ways* (Canterbury Press, 2003), *Re-pitching the Tent: The Definitive Guide to Reordering Church Buildings for Worship and Mission* (Canterbury Press, third edition 2004), *Creating Uncommon Worship: Transforming the Liturgy of the Eucharist* (Canterbury Press, 2004), *Always Open: Being Anglican Today* (2005), *Mark My Word* (second edition 2005), *Here I Am: Reflections on the Ordained Life* (Canterbury Press, 2006) and *Times and Seasons: Creating Transformative Worship Throughout the Year* (Canterbury Press, 2008).

Nicola Slee is Research Fellow and Co-ordinator of the MA in Applied Theology at the Queen's Foundation for Ecumenical Theological Education, Birmingham. Her publications include *Faith and Feminism: An Introduction to Christian Feminist Theology* (2003), *Women's*

Faith Development: Patterns and Processes (2004), *Praying Like a Woman* (2004), *Doing December Differently: An Alternative Christmas Handbook* (co-edited with Rosie Miles, 2006), *The Book of Mary* (2007) and *The Edge of God: New Liturgical Texts and Contexts in Conversation* (co-edited with Michael Jagessar and Stephen Burns, 2008).

Ann Loades, CBE, is Emerita Professor of Divinity and Professorial Fellow at St Chad's College, Durham University . She is also Lay Canon of Durham Cathedral and a member of the Church of England's Doctrine Commission. Her publications include *Searching for Lost Coins: Explorations in Christianity and Feminism* (1987), *Feminist Theology: A Reader* (ed., 1990), *Dorothy L. Sayers: Spiritual Writings* (ed., 1993), *Spiritual Classics from the Late Twentieth Century* (ed., 1995), *The Sense of the Sacramental: Movement and Measure in Art and Music, Space and Time* (co-edited with David Brown, 1995), *Christ: The Sacramental Word* (co-edited with David Brown, 1996), *Evelyn Underhill* (1997), *Feminist Theology: Voices from the Past* (2001), *The Truth-Seeking Heart: Austin Farrer and his Writings* (co-edited with Robert MacSwain, Canterbury Press, 2006), and the series *Problems in Theology* (co-edited with Jeff Astley and David Brown, 2003–).

Mark Ireland is Vicar of All Saints, Wellington, with St Catherine's, Eyton, in the Diocese of Lichfield. He was formerly Diocesan Missioner for the Diocese of Lichfield. His publications include *Evangelism: Which Way Now?* (with Mike Booker, second edition 2005) and *Evangelism in a Spiritual Age* (with Steven Croft and others, 2005).

Stephen Burns is Research Fellow in Public and Contextual Theology at the United Theological College, Charles Sturt University, Sydney, NSW, Australia. He is a priest in the Diocese of Canberra and Goulburn. His publications include *Worship in Context: Liturgical Theology, Children and the City* (2006), *Liturgy* (SCM Studyguide, 2006), *Exchanges of Grace: Essays in Honour of Ann Loades* (co-edited with Natalie K. Watson, 2008) and *The Edge of God: New Liturgical Texts and Contexts in Conversation* (co-edited with Michael Jagessar and Nicola Slee, 2008).